The General Unified
Theory of Intelligence

The General Unified Theory of Intelligence

Its Central Conceptions and Specific
Application to Domains
of Cognitive Science

Morton Wagman

Westport, Connecticut
London

Library of Congress Cataloging-in-Publication Data

Wagman, Morton.
    The general unified theory of intelligence : its central
conceptions and specific application to domains of cognitive science
/ Morton Wagman.
        p.   cm.
    Includes bibliographical references and index.
    ISBN 0-275-95622-9 (alk. paper)
    1. Intellect. 2. Cognitive Science. 3. Artificial intelligence.
4. Cognition. I. Title.
  BF431.W2   1997
  153.9—dc20   96-20708

British Library Cataloguing in Publication Data is available.

Library of Congress Catalog Card Number: 96-20708
ISBN: 0-275-95622-9

First published in 1997

Praeger Publishers, 88 Post Road West, Westport, CT 06881
An imprint of Greenwood Publishing Group, Inc.

Printed in the United States of America

∞™

The paper used in this book complies with the
Permanent Paper Standard issued by the National
Information Standards Organization (Z39.48-1984).

10 9 8 7 6 5 4 3 2 1

Copyright Acknowledgments

The author and publisher gratefully acknowledge permission to use extracts from the following materials.

Holyoak, K.J. and Spellman, B.A. (1993). Thinking. *Annual Review of Psychology,* 44:265–315. Reproduced, with permission, from the *Annual Review of Psychology,* Volume 44: 1993, by Annual Reviews, Inc.

Holyoak, K.J. and Thagard, P. (1989). Analogical mapping by constraint satisfaction. *Cognitive Science, 13*:295–355. Reprinted with the permission of Ablex Publishing Corporation.

Langley, P. (1981). Data-driven discovery of physical laws. *Cognitive Science,* 5:31–54. Reprinted with the permission of Ablex Publishing Corporation.

Rosenbloom, P.S., Laird, J.E., Newell, A. and McCarl, R. (1991). A preliminary analysis of the SOAR architecture as a basis for general intelligence. *Artificial Intelligence,* 47:289–325. Reprinted with the permission of Elsevier Science Publishers.

Smith, E.E., Langston, C. and Nisbett, R.E. (1992). The case for rules in reasoning. *Cognitive Science, 16*:1–40. Reprinted with the permission of Ablex Publishing Corporation.

Sternberg, R.J. (1990). *Metaphors of Mind: Conceptions of the Nature of Intelligence.* Cambridge, England: Cambridge University Press. Reprinted with the permission of Cambridge University Press and R.J. Sternberg.

Thagard, P. (1989). Explanatory coherence. *Behavioral and Brain Sciences, 12*:435–502. Reprinted with the permission of Cambridge University Press and Paul Thagard.

Wagman, M. (1991). *Cognitive Science and Concepts of Mind: Toward a General Unified Theory of Intelligence.* New York: Praeger. Reprinted with the permission of Praeger Publishers.

Wagman, M. (1993). *Cognitive Psychology and Artificial Intelligence: Theory and Research in Cognitive Science.* New York: Praeger. Reprinted with the permission of Praeger Publishers.

Wagman, M. (1995). *The Sciences of Cognition: Theory and Research in Psychology and Artificial Intelligence.* New York: Praeger. Reprinted with the permission of Praeger Publishers.

Contents

Illustrations

FIGURE

Preface

The general unified theory of intelligence centers on thinking, reasoning, and problem solving and minimally on sensory motor processes. More specifically, the general unified theory of intelligence focuses on the generality of theories and models of deductive, inductive, analogical, and explanatory reasoning and places special emphasis on theories, models, and architectures that are inclusive of humans and computers and thereby constitute unified conceptions of intelligence.

At an abstract level, the general unified theory of intelligence construes the intellective functions of humans and computers as restricted and directed forms of implication: conditional reasoning in the case of humans and production rules in the case of computers. These abstract conceptions are developed at length in the first chapter of the book. The next six chapters examine the research and conceptual ramifications of the ideas contained in chapter one. In the eighth and final chapter, the major themes developed in the book are summarized and conclusions are drawn regarding the validity, scope, and limitations of the general unified theory of intelligence.

In the first chapter, the central place of the logic of implication in the general unified theory of intelligence is discussed in detail. The logic of implication is a bridging concept between human and artificial intelligence. Logical implication is related to mathematical proof, production system, Turing's theory of computation, the psychology of reasoning, Gödel's theorem, representational theory in artificial intelligence, the resolution method in artificial intelligence, and the psychological content of implication statements. The chapter also discusses unified theories in science, the nature of intelligence, and the limits of logic, mathematics, and theories of intelligence.

In the second chapter, the theme of logical implication introduced in the first chapter is developed by considering the generality with which abstract rules (types of implication) are employed in everyday human reasoning. A set of criteria, derived from experimental research, demonstrates that abstract rules are used in permission, obligation, causal, statistical, and modus ponens reasoning.

In the third chapter, the creative mechanisms by which BACON.3 achieves the rediscovery of a set of scientific laws are set forth. The creative mechanisms are sophisticated productions rules (a type of implication). These creative mechanisms are illustrated by BACON.3's rediscovery of Kepler's third law of planetary motion. BACON.3's mode of rediscovery is compared with rediscovery by university students in a laboratory setting and with Kepler's original discovery. A discussion of the generality of scientific discovery processes concludes the chapter.

In the fourth chapter, computational approaches to analogical thinking are described. The ACME program uses parallel constraint satisfaction to achieve intelligent mapping between source and target analogs. The generality of ACME is demonstrated across a number of domains including a mathematical analogy and a literary metaphor. In the second part of the chapter, a general componential theory of analogical reasoning applicable to humans and computers is discussed in depth.

In the fifth chapter, a theory of explanatory coherence is presented. The theory is implemented in the ECHO system that evaluates competing theories and hypotheses in a connectionist architecture that employs a parallel constraint satisfaction algorithm. The generality of ECHO is demonstrated in a series of applications that range across scientific theory and everyday reasoning.

In the sixth chapter, symbolic-connectionist architectures are described. These computational models are directed toward providing an integrated account of both strategic and automatic cognitive processes that constitute general human intelligence.

In the seventh chapter, the SOAR system is described. Using production rules (a type of implication), SOAR is an ongoing research program that is intended to provide a unified theory of human cognition.

In the eighth and final chapter, major themes discussed in the book are summarized and conclusions regarding the general unified theory of intelligence are presented.

The book is intended for scholars and professionals in psychology, artifical intelligence, and cognitive science. Graduate and advanced undergraduate students in these and related disciplines will also find the book useful.

I wish to thank LaDonna Wilson for her outstanding assistance in the preparation of all aspects of the manuscript.

General Unified Theory of Intelligence

Central Aspects of the Theory

A different, more abstract, and inclusive general unified theory of intelligence can be formulated on the basis of the logic of implication. This fundamental theorem of intelligence would hold that the logic of implication (if p, then q) subsumes both the formal structure of human reasoning and problem solving, and the formal structure of artificial intelligence. The logic of implication is foundational to mathematical and scientific reasoning and to the reasoning of everyday behavior as well (Wagman, 1978, 1984, 1993), and is foundational to programming logic and knowledge representation formalisms in artificial intelligence systems (Wagman, 1980, 1988, 1991a, l991b).

Mathematics and Unified Theories in Science

Mathematics summarizes scientific research results; more significantly, it formulates general bodies of scientific theory.

> Mathematics is the foundation of all exact knowledge of natural phenomena [Hilbert, quoted in Kline, 1985, p. vi].

Unified Electromagnetic Theory

The mathematical equations of Maxwell constitute the complete and precise formulation of the theory of electromagnetism. An immense range of physical phenomena are unified mathematically.

The mathematical equations have profound significance. The equations unify the diverse phenomena in the radiation spectrum, end deductions from the equations describe and predict empirical results of experiments and applications. Physical explanation is by means of mathematical symbols.

> In Maxwell's theory an electric charge is but the recipient of a symbol [Helmholtz, quoted in Kline, 1985, p. 146].

> The originality of mathematics consists in the fact that in mathematical sciences connections between things are exhibited which, apart from the agency of human reason, are extremely unobvious [Whitehead, quoted in Kline, 1985, p. 141].

Unified Newtonian Theory

The Newtonian theory is a mathematical theory that describes and predicts by means of its equations the terrestrial and celestial behavior of physical bodies. The mathematical equations and deductions from them are universal. Newton's equations for the force of attraction between two masses include a gravitational constant, but the concept of gravitation itself is not well understood.

The Newtonian equations and their derivations are basic to the contemporary scientific exploration of space, but their extraordinary scope and power were already known in the eighteenth-century mathematical work of Lagrange and Laplace.

> The application of . . . principles to the motions of the heavenly bodies had conducted us, by geometrical reasoning, without any hypothesis, to the law of universal attraction, the action of gravity and the motion of projectiles being particular cases of this law. . . . From these expressions we have deduced . . . the precision of the equinoxes; the libration of the moon; and the figure and rotation of Saturn's rings [Laplace, quoted in Kline, 1985, p. 119].

Regarding the law of gravitation, Newton himself emphasized that it was a mathematical law, a computational law, and not one based on the complete knowledge of gravitation itself:

> So far I have explained the phenomena of the heavens and of the sea by the force of gravity. . . . I have not yet been able to deduce from the phenomena the reasons for these properties of gravity and I invent no hypothesis [*hypotheses no fingo*]. For everything which is not deduced from the phenomena should be called a hypothesis, and hypotheses, whether metaphysical or physical, whether occult qualities or mechanical, have no

place in experimental philosophy. In this philosophy propositions are deduced from phenomena and rendered general by induction. . . . It is enough that gravity really exists, that it acts according to the laws we have set out and that it suffices for all the movements of the heavenly bodies and of the sea [Newton, quoted in Kline, 1985, p. 121].

Unified Einsteinian Theory

Einsteinian theory subsumes Newtonian theory. However, the concept of weight due to gravitational force is eliminated. Mass is considered as inertial mass in the two Newtonian equations.

The Newtonian concept of three-dimensional Euclidean space is replaced by curved, four-dimensional space-time. In Einsteinian theory, observed measurements may vary as a function of the relative location of the observer and relative motions of frames of reference. The mathematical theory involves equations of Reimannian differential geometry and the equations of tensor analysis; the former relate to the nature of Einsteinian space, the latter to the equalization of varying observers and frames of reference. Tensor analysis provided Einstein with a mathematical basis for his unified theory of relativity: "The general laws of nature are to be expressed by equations which hold good for all systems of coordinates" (Einstein, quoted in Kline, 1985, p. 163).

Logical Structure and the Reality of the General Unified Theory of Intelligence

The architecture of the general unified theory of intelligence is constructed on the foundation stone of the logic of implication that supports conceptual elements in both natural intelligence and artificial intelligence. The architecture coordinates a remote abstract logical structure on the one hand and the palpable evidential behavior of human and computer reasoning and problem-solving on the other hand. The concrete reality of the latter is brought under the explanatory aegis of the former. Mathematical logical symbols preside over, and give the best explanation of, cognition. This precedence of logic seems counterintuitive; yet there is a clear and illuminating analogy in the relationship between logic and physics as summarized by Albert Einstein (1931):

According to Newton's system, physical reality is characterized by the concepts of space, time, material point, and force (reciprocal action of material points. . . .

After Maxwell they conceived physical reality as represented by continuous fields, not mechanically explicable, which are subject to partial differential equations. This change in the conception of reality is the most profound and fruitful one that has come to physics since Newton. . . .

The view I have just outlined of the purely fictitious character of the fundamentals of scientific theory was by no means the prevailing one in the 18th and 19th centuries. But it is steadily gaining ground from the fact that *the distance in thought between the fundamental concepts and laws on one side, and, on the other, the conclusions which have to be brought into relation with our experience grows larger and larger, the simpler the logical structure becomes—that is to say, the smaller the number of logically independent conceptual elements which are found necessary to support the structure* [italics added].

The Intelligence of Mathematics

The ancient Pythagoreans proclaimed with awe "All is number." Heinrich Hertz, who developed the theory and technology of radio waves, asserted that electromagnetic wave phenomena were best understood as mathematical equations and, like Pythagoras, believed that mathematics had an intrinsic intelligence of its own that sometimes surpassed its creators.

Hertz said, "Maxwell's theory consists of Maxwell's equations" (quoted in Kline, 1985, p. 144). There is no mechanical explanation, and there is no need for one.

One cannot escape the feeling that these equations have an existence and an intelligence of their own, that they are wiser than we are, even than their discoverers, that we get more out of them than we originally put in to them [Hertz, quoted in Kline, 1980, p. 338].

Logical Implication and Mathematical Proof

The first known application of the logical implication argument known as "reductio ad absurdum" to the establishment of mathematical proofs was made by Euclid around 300 B.C. In the reductio ad absurdum argument, there are three steps in the establishment of the truth of a mathematical proposition: (a) assume the proposition is false, (b) demonstrate that the implication of this assumption leads to a contradiction, and (c) conclude on the ground of the contradiction that the proposition is true. Euclid used this method to establish the truth of the following proposition: The square root of two is an irrational number.

During the centuries following Euclid, mathematicians have established the truth or falsehood of many mathematical conjectures by means of the reductio ad absurdum argument.

In 1993, the mathematical conjecture known as "Fermat's last theorem" was proven to be true (Kolata, 1993). Fermat had advanced his conjecture in the seventeenth century but its establishment had eluded generations of the world's best mathematicians. Fermat proposed that the equation $x^n + y^n = z^n$, where x, y, and z are integers, has no solution for values of n greater than two.

In a lecture given at Cambridge University before an assemblage of renowned mathematicians in June 1993, Professor Andrew Wiles of Princeton University proved by means of the reductio ad absurdum argument that Fermat's conjecture was true.

Clearly, the establishment of Professor Wiles's proof, like the establishment of Euclid's proof, required, in addition to the reductio ad absurdum method, technical mathematical knowledge (elementary algebra in the case of Euclid, advanced algebraic geometry and other topics in the case of Professor Wiles). The reductio ad absurdum argument is, however, a sine qua non.

The Intelligence of Computer Programs

In their proof of the Four Color Theorem, Appel and Haken (1979) found, to their surprise, that their computer program made intellectual contributions to their complex work and displayed an original intelligence that sometimes surpassed their own.

In early 1975 we modified [the] experimental program to yield obstacle-free configurations and forced it to search for arguments that employed configurations of small ring size. The resulting runs pointed out the need for new improvements in the procedure, but also yielded a very pleasant surprise: replacing geographically good configurations by obstacle-free ones did not seem to more than double the size of the unavoidable set.

At this point the program, which has by now absorbed our ideas and improvements for two years, began to surprise us. At the beginning we would check its arguments by hand so we could always predict the course it would follow in any situation; but now it suddenly started to act like a chess-playing machine. It would work out compound strategies based on all the tricks it had been "taught" and often these approaches were far more clever than those we would have tried. Thus it began to teach us things about how to proceed that we never expected. In a sense it had surpassed its creators in some aspects of the "intellectual" as well as the mechanical parts of the task [Appel and Haken, 1979, p. 175, italics added].

Intelligence and Nature

The work of Newton, Maxwell, and Einstein has rendered nature mathematically comprehensible. Inherent in mathematics and in computer programs there appears to be, as discussed in the previous two sections, an order of intelligence that "is wiser than we are, wiser even than their discoverers" (Hertz) and that "surpassed its creators in some aspects of the intellectual as well as the mechanical parts of the task" (Appel and Haken). The human mind has created both mathematical intelligence and artificial intelligence, and though these creations may seem to provide inevitable and singular truths about nature, these truths are arbitrary constructions and the result of our own cognitive projections.

> [We] have found that where science has progressed the farthest, the mind has but regained from nature that which the mind has put into nature. We have found a strange footprint on the shore of the unknown. We have devised profound theories, one after another, to account for its origin. At last, we have succeeded in reconstructing the creature that made the footprint. And Lo! it is our own [Eddington, 1933].

It is of interest that Sir Arthur Stanley Eddington (1882–1944), who in 1919 confirmed by astronomical measurements predictions derived from Einstein's theory of relativity, hypothesized that since knowledge of the universe is the product of the human mind, discovery of the nature of the mechanics of the human mind would enable purely conceptual procedures to formulate the entire science of physics.

Eddington constructed his hypothesis long before developments in cognitive psychology and artificial intelligence resulted in specific knowledge of the operations of the human mind. These advances in cognitive science have impressed the eminent theoretical physicist Stephen Hawking to further Eddington's hypothesis and turn it in the unexpected direction wherein computer programs rather than human minds create theoretical physics.

> At present computers are a useful aid in research but they have to be directed by human minds. However, if one extrapolates their recent rapid rate of development, it would seem quite possible that they will take over altogether in theoretical physics. So maybe the end is in sight for theoretical physicists if not for theoretical physics [Hawking, quoted in Davis and Hersh, 1986, p. 158].

Logical Implication and Production System

It is important to distinguish logical implication from the similar-appearing production system or production rule. Logical implication is concerned with propositions and their truths. A production rule is concerned with the action to be taken when conditions are met. In logical implication, the validity of deductive reasoning can be guaranteed if the rules of predicate logic are followed. In a production system, the actions taken when conditions are met may be practically useful or appropriate, but the executed procedure carries no guarantee. The symbolic expression or formula for a logical implication is as follows: $P_1 \ldots P_n \subset Q$. In ordinary English, it is true that propositions $P_1 \ldots P_n$ imply proposition Q. The symbolic expression or formula for a production rule is $C_1 \ldots C_n > A$. In ordinary English, under conditions $C_1 \ldots C_n$ do action A. The essential nature of a production rule is that it is a command so that $C > A$ is to be followed even when A is "conclude Q." Production rules have the character of imperative procedures in contrast to logical implication concerned with the truth or falsity of propositions.

Logical Implication and Turing's Theory of Computation

At the beginning of this section, I indicated the central place that logical implication has in my general unified theory of natural and artificial intelligence. Modern programming languages such as PROLOG are applications of the logic of implication (Kowalski, 1979). The truth-functional character of logical implication constitutes the formal representation of the two most basic procedural operations of the Turing machine. I express the formal representation of these operations as (1) $P_0 \subset Q_1$, (2) $P_1 \subset Q_0$.

The Turing machine, an abstract computer (Turing, 1936), can be briefly described as follows:

A Turing machine consists of two primary (theoretical) units: a "tape drive" and a "computation unit." The tape drive has a tape of infinite length on which there can be written (and subsequently read) any series of two symbols: 0 (zero) and 1 (one). The computation unit contains a program that consists of a sequence of commands made up from the list of operations below. Each "command" consists of two specified operations, one to be followed if the last symbol read by the machine was a 0 and one if it has just read a 1. Below are the Turing machine operations:

> Read tape
> Move tape left
> Move tape right
> Write 0 in the tape
> Write 1 on the tape
> Jump to another command
> Halt

[Kurzweil, 1990, p. 112].

Computation Theory and Intelligence

Turing's *mathematical proofs* (1936) concerning the universal Turing machine that can simulate the performance of any conceivable computer, the existence of problems that can never be solved but are known to possess unique solutions, and the existence of infinitely equal unsolvable problems and solvable problems must be sharply delineated from Turing's *psychological conjecture* (Turing, 1950) that the human brain and its intelligence are computationally tractable and subsumable under the mathematical theory of the universal Turing machine. Turing's proposal of "the imitation game" as a test of parity between computer intelligence and human intelligence is an inadequate criterion of his psychological conjecture, whose limits must be tested by the usual procedures of science. The computability of the brain and its intelligence must stand or fall in the outcome of empirical inquiry into neural and cognitive processes.

Limits of Logic, Mathematics and Theories of Intelligence

Systems of logic and mathematics have theoretical limits as proved by Turing (1936), Church (1956), and Gödel (1931). In sufficiently complex systems of logic and mathematics, there exist propositions that are definitely true or definitely false, but which of these two truth values is correct can never be established with certainty. These limits apply to theories of intelligence both natural and artificial.

Logical Implication and Psychology of Reasoning

As a formal symbolic structure, logical implication is a regular constituent of computational intelligence and a staple of university courses in symbolic logic. In everyday reasoning, people depend on the inferential strength of logical implication, but they do not reason their way through everyday problems by manipulating the predicate calculus symbols that represent logical implication (Wagman, 1978, 1984). Instead, they use pragmatic forms of implication (if, then) and ordinary language (Leahey and Wagman, 1974; Wagman, 1979, 1980). The symbols of logical implication, like the symbols of algebra, possess a great generality because of their abstract character, but specific applications of the logic of implication or the mathematics of algebra will entail specific contexts and specific meanings. The psychological application of logical implication has been investigated by Cheng and Holyoak (1985), and their work has been summarized by Hunt (1989) as follows:

> Cheng and Holyoak (1985) brought the study of generalized reasoning schemes into the laboratory. They showed that the logical connective "implication" is, psychologically, represented by several different "pragmatic reasoning schemas." One is the permission schema: If A occurs then B is permitted (e.g., "If a traveler is inoculated, then the traveler may enter the country"). Another is obligation: If A has happened, then the actor

must do B (e.g., "In order to use the library you must have a card"). Both schemas are examples of implication. Psychologically, however, the conditions indicating the applicability of causal and permission schemas are different [p. 619].

Logical Implication: Gödel and Artificial Intelligence

Logical implication was central to Gödel's analytical proof of his famous mathematical theorems. Gödel's theorems, which place limits on the logical completeness and consistency of mathematical systems, have sometimes been interpreted as placing unique limits on artificial intelligence.

The equivalence of provability and logical implication was first proved by Gödel (Gödel, 1930); proofs appear in textbooks on logic. The incompleteness of any infinite axiomatization of arithmetic also was proved by Gödel (Gödel, 1931). Although this result is extremely important in mathematical logic, *it does not* (as some people have claimed [Lucas, 1961]) *preclude the possibility that machines will be able to reason as well as people* [italics added]. People cannot prove consistency of complex systems in this way either! [Genesereth and Nilsson, 1987, p. 62].

Mathematical proofs have sometimes been used to demonstrate that there are limits to the powers of artificial intelligence, in general, and of computers in particular (Dreyfus, 1972). For example, Gödel's theorem (1931) demonstrates that for any sufficiently complex logical system, propositions can be stated that can neither be disproved nor proved within that system, without the system itself being logically inconsistent. However, the application of Gödel's theorem to demonstrate theoretical limits of computers equally extends to demonstrate theoretical limits to the powers of human intelligence. In any case, Gödel's theorem has not impeded advances in the field of mathematics, nor should it impede advances in the field of artificial intelligence (Wagman, 1988, p. 11).

Production Rules as Theoretical Constructs

In cognitive psychology and artificial intelligence, production rules are theoretical variables that control the representation and processing of information or knowledge. The role of production rules in the human information processing system and their distinction from the stimulus-response variables or behaviors are set forth in accounts by Newell (1990) and Anderson (1983).

Logical Implication: Production System and Representation in Artificial Intelligence

The general unified theory of intelligence describes the concept of production system as an implementation of logical implication. In turn, the production system concept is fundamental in artificial intelligence in that the many distinct methods of knowledge representation in artificial intelligence can all be reduced to the theory of production systems.

A production system consists of

> —A set of rules, each consisting of a left side (a pattern) that determines the applicability of the rule and a right side that describes the operation to be performed if the rule is applied.
> —One or more knowledge/databases that contain whatever information is appropriate for the particular task. Some parts of the database may be permanent, while other parts of it may pertain only to the solution of the current problem. *The information in these databases may be structured in any appropriate way* [Rich and Knight, 1991, p. 36, italics added].

> Post (1943) provided a mathematical demonstration that any representational formalism in artificial intelligence can be subsumed under the theory of the production system [Wagman, 1991, p. 62].

Logical Implication: The Resolution Method in Artificial Intelligence

Logical implication in the form of a reductio ad absurdum argument is important in the classic artificial intelligence method of resolution.

> In a way we may regard Euclid's method of proof as foreshadowing the development of the general resolution theory of theorem-proving in artificial intelligence (Robinson, 1965). Thus, Euclid's use of the logical deduction law *reductio ad absurdum* to prove that the square root of two is an irrational number . . . is echoed in Robinson's use of *reductio ad absurdum* as the central logical mechanism by which artificial intelligence accomplished the goal of mathematical theorem proving and general problem solving (Cheng and Juang, 1987; Genesereth, 1983).
>
> The powerful mathematical reasoning method of *reductio ad absurdum,* as used by many creative mathematicians (including Alan Turing) to establish the proof of a proposition or theorem, consists of a sequential logical procedure. The sequence begins with the assumption that the proposition or theorem is false, continues with mathematical deductions that follow from the initial assumption, and concludes with a demonstration that these deductions culminate in the contradiction of the initial assumption that the proposition or theorem was false. . . .

Resolution is used to prove theorems that are written in the predicate calculus (Chang and Lee, 1973). The predicate calculus, in turn, represents a state of affairs or problem state. Proving the theorem becomes equivalent to problem solving.

Contradiction or refutation is the goal in theorem-proving by the general resolution method. Contradiction or refutation proves the falsity of the negation of a proposition and thus establishes its truth. . . .

The general strategy of resolution in a theorem-proving system involves a set of procedures that begins with the representation of a state of affairs in the language of the predicate calculus. . . . The predicate calculus expressions are rewritten as groupings of logic symbols, termed clauses. . . . The inference rules of resolution are then applied to the clauses. . . .

These inference rules are directed toward a gradual simplification of the set of clauses (in large systems, thousands of clauses may be involved [Clocksin and Mellish, 1981]). Simplification involves the conversion, by means of rules of logic, . . . of conjunctions into disjunctions and implications into disjunctions. Resolution is then applied to disjunctive clauses that are complementary in sign. These pairs of clauses are then resolved, that is, eliminated from the set of clauses. The process continues with the elimination of further clauses until the nil . . . or empty clause is produced (no complementary disjunctions remain). . . .

The resolution method is designed to enable computer systems to solve problems by theorem proving. The logic of the theorem-proving and the resolution by refutation or contradiction can be briefly summarized.

From a set of propositions, prove some goal X. The first step is to negate the goal X. The second step is to add the negation of X to the set of propositions, thus forming an expanded set. The third step is to transform the expanded set of propositions into a set of clauses (groupings of predicate calculus expressions).

The fourth step is to apply resolution to the set of clauses with the intended purpose of deriving a contradiction (the nil clauses). From the contradiction, the final logical step is the negation of the negation of the goal X; that is, the proof of the theorem is established [Wagman, 1991, pp. 41–46].

The Formal Core of Types of Implication Statements

Implication statements may be of different types but they have a formal core. The formal core abstracts the essence of the relationship between the antecedent and consequent parts of the implication statement. As an abstraction, the formal core ignores some of the distinctive meaning of the type of implication. The valid formal core of an implication statement requires that it is not the case both that the antecedent is true and that the consequent is false. Types of implication statements include logical conditionals, definitional conditionals, causal conditionals, and decisional conditionals. Conditionals are ordinarily expressed as if-then statements and their content is indefinitely varied, but their formal validity is singularly determined by the criterion stated earlier.

Logical Form Versus Psychological Content

The nature of logic is often misunderstood by research psychologists. The misunderstanding centers around three characteristics of logic that separate it as a discipline from psychology. First, logic is concerned with validity of argument and not with truth or content of the argument. Second, logic is abstract and formal in that it is concerned with variables and rules of inference and not with psychological behavior and everyday reasoning. Third, logic is concerned only with the minimum condition necessary to establish validity and not with the many conditions, contexts, and contents of psychological experience and behavior.

Problem Solving and Conceptions of Human and Artificial Intelligence

Intelligence is most frequently construed as successful adaptation. Adaptation requires finding satisfactory solutions to problems. Therefore, definitions, theories, and assessments of intelligence, academic, practical, and social, from the time of the first symposium on intelligence (1921) to the second symposium on intelligence (1986) have regularly underscored the salience of problem-solving acumen. Data concerning these symposia on intelligence are presented in Table 1.1 and are commented on by Sternberg (1990) in the following passage.

Comparison of the 1921 and 1986 symposia

In order to understand how definitions of intelligence have evolved, Cynthia Berg and I attempted to trace the evolution of the concept of intelligence from the 1921 to the 1986 symposium. [Table 1.1] lists twenty-seven attributes that appeared in the present and past definitions of intelligence and their frequencies in each of the two symposia. The small number of listings for each attribute would render formal statistical analysis hazardous. But some generalizations can nevertheless be made.

First, at least some general agreement exists across the two symposia regarding the nature of intelligence. The correlation between the two sets of frequencies is .50, indicating moderate overlap in present and past conceptions. *Attributes such as adaptation to the environment, basic mental processes, and higher order thinking (e.g., reasoning, problem solving, decision making) were prominent in both listings.*

Second, certain themes recur in both symposia. The issue of the one versus the many—Is intelligence one thing or is it manifold?—continues to be of concern, although no consensus exists upon this matter. The issue of breadth of definition also continues to be of concern. As in the earlier

TABLE 1.1

Frequencies of Attributes that Contributors Used to Define Intelligence in 1986 and 1921.

		1986		1921	
		No.	%	No.	%
1.	Adaptation, in order to meet the demands of the environment effectively	3	13	4	29
2.	Elementary processes (perception, sensation, attention)	5	21	3	21
3.	Metacognition (knowledge about cognition)	4	17	1	7
4.	Executive processes	6	25	1	7
5.	Interaction of processes and knowledge	4	17	0	0
6.	Higher level components (abstract reasoning, represent- ation, problem solving, decision making)	12	50	8	57
7.	Knowledge	5	21	1	7
8.	Ability to learn	4	17	4	29
9.	Physiological mechanisms	2	8	4	29
10.	Discrete set of abilities (e.g., spatial, verbal, auditory)	4	17	1	7
11.	Speed of mental processing	3	13	2	14
12.	Automated performance	3	13	0	0
13.	g	4	17	2	14
14.	Real-world manifestations (social, practical, tacit)	2	8	0	0
15.	That which is valued by culture	7	29	0	0
16.	Not easily definable, not one construct	4	17	2	14
17.	A field of scholarship	1	4	0	0
18.	Capacities prewired at birth	3	13	1	7
19.	Emotional, motivational constructs	1	4	1	7
20.	Restricted to academic/cognitive abilities	2	8	2	14
21.	Individual differences in mental competence	1	4	0	0
22.	Generation of environment based on genetic programming	1	4	0	0
23.	Ability to deal with novelty	1	4	1	7
24.	Mental playfulness	1	4	0	0
25.	Only important in its predictive value	0	0	1	7
26.	Inhibitive capacity	0	0	1	7
27.	Overt behavioral manifestation (effective/ successful responses)	5	21	3	21

Source: Sternberg, 1990, p. 50.

symposium, some panelists define intelligence quite narrowly in terms of biological or, especially, cognitive elements, whereas others include a broader array of elements, including motivation and personality. The issue of breadth, like that of the one versus the many, remains unresolved. Investigators still disagree as to the relative emphasis that should be placed in theory and research upon physiological versus behavioral manifestations of intelligence, and the respective roles of process and product in defining intelligence also remain unresolved.

Third, despite the similarities in views over the 65 years, some salient differences in the two listings can also be found. Metacognition—conceived of as both knowledge about and control of cognition—plays a prominent role in the 1986 symposium but virtually no role at all in the 1921 symposium. The salience of metacognition and executive processes can undoubtedly be attributed to the predominance of the computer metaphor in the current study of cognition and in information processing approaches to intelligence. In the present symposium, a greater emphasis has been placed on the role of knowledge and the interaction between this knowledge and mental processes. The change in emphasis is not entirely with respect to functions that occur within the organism. The present panelists show considerable emphasis on the role of context, and particularly of culture, in defining intelligence, whereas such emphasis was absent in the earlier symposium. . . .

To summarize, the field of intelligence has evolved from one that concentrated primarily on psychometric issues in 1921 to one that concentrates primarily on information processing, cultural context, and their interrelationships in 1986. Prediction of behavior seems to be somewhat less important than the understanding of that behavior, which needs to precede prediction. On one hand, few if any issues about the nature of intelligence have been truly resolved. On the other hand, investigators of intelligence seem to have come a rather long way toward understanding the cognitive and cultural bases for the test scores since 1921 [Sternberg, 1990, pp. 49–53, italics added].

Paralleling human intelligence, problem solving is a central capacity of artificial intelligence systems. These systems are essential to the solution of highly complex scientific and technical problems.

The computational systems and the human systems are intelligent, as they both possess intellectual confidence and deploy their confidence in successful adaptation or problem solving.

In the general unified theory of intelligence, problem solving in the case of human intelligence applies the logic of implication (if, then); in the case of artificial intelligence it applies the logic of implication in the form of production rules (condition, action). The abstract unity of human and artificial intelligence rests on the theory of logical implication.

2

The Generality of Abstract Rules in Intelligent Reasoning

A central issue in comparing human and artificial reasoning concerns the employment of abstract rules of inference. Clearly, insofar as artificial intelligence employs the predicate calculus, its reasoning is abstract. It is also the case that logicians and mathematicians in their formal professional work use systems of deductive inference. But do they and people in general employ abstract rules in everyday reasoning and problem solving? This important question was addressed by Smith, Langston, and Nisbett (1992):

> A number of theoretical positions in psychology—including variants of case-based reasoning, instance-based analogy, and connectionist models—maintain that abstract rules are not involved in human reasoning, or at best play a minor role. Other views hold that the use of abstract rules is a core aspect of human reasoning. We propose eight criteria for determining whether or not people use abstract rules in reasoning, and examine evidence relevant to each criterion for several rule systems. We argue that there is substantial evidence that several different inferential rules, including modus ponens, contractual rules, and the law of large numbers, are used in solving everyday problems. We discuss the implications for various theoretical positions and consider hybrid mechanisms that combine aspects of instance and rule models [p. 1].

Smith, Langston, and Nisbett (1992) state their general methodology in the following terms:

We propose eight criteria for deciding whether a given abstract rule is applied, where each criterion essentially embodies a phenomenon that is more readily explained by a rule-based approach than by an alternative model. We argue that use of these criteria indicates there is substantial evidence for people's use of several deductive and inductive inferential rules, all of which have in common that they are widely considered to be normatively required for correct reasoning [p. 2].

The First Criterion of Rule Use

The first criterion and its rationale are presented in the following account.

Criterion 1: Performance on Rule-Governed Items Is as Accurate with Unfamiliar as with Familiar Items.

Rationale. The logic behind Criterion 1 stems from the idea that an abstract rule is applicable to a specific item because the item can be represented by some *special abstract structure* that also defines the rule (the special structure is the antecedent part of the rule). Because even novel items can possess this special structure, they can be assimilated to the rule (see Rips, 1990). . . .

When a test item or problem is presented, it is coded in a form that is *sufficiently abstract* to lead to access of an abstract rule: Once accessed, if need be, the rule can be used for further abstract coding of the test item. The next stage is to instantiate, or bind, the variables in the rule with entities from the input. Finally, the rule is applied to yield the desired answer; that is, inspection of the instantiated representation reveals that the antecedent of the rule has been satisfied, thereby licensing the conclusion. There are therefore four stages: coding, access, instantiation (variable binding), and application.

We can illustrate the model with our "If gork then flum; gork; ?" example. When presented with this item, you might code it, in part, as an "If X, then Y" type item. This would suffice to access modus ponens. Next, you would instantiate p with "gork" and q with "flum." Then you would apply the rule and derive "flum" as an answer. Note that had you initially coded the item more superficially—say, as an "If-then claim"—this might still have sufficed to activate modus ponens, which could then have been used to elaborate the abstract coding. Though this is merely a sketch of a model, it is compatible with the general structure of rule-based models of deductive and inductive reasoning (e.g., Collins and Michalski, 1989; Rips, 1983).

With this sketch in hand we can be more explicit about how our criterion of equivalent accuracy for familiar and unfamiliar items fits with rule-following. If we assume that there is no effect of familiarity on the likelihood of coding an item sufficiently abstractly, then there will be no effect of familiarity on the likelihood of accessing an abstract rule. Similarly, if we assume there is no effect of familiarity on instantiating a rule or inspecting an instantiated representation, there will be no effect of familiarity on applying a rule. Both assumptions seem plausible, which makes the criterion plausible (i.e., familiar items should not lead to greater accuracy). Indeed, if anything, the more familiar an item is, the *less* likely it is to be coded abstractly. This is because familiarity often rests on frequency, and frequent presentations of an item might lead one to represent it in terms of its specific content.

For a criterion to be truly useful, of course, the phenomenon it describes must also be difficult to account for by a non-rule-based explanation. The major alternatives to rule models are instance models, and Criterion 1 is indeed hard to explain in terms of instances. To appreciate this point, consider a rough sketch of a prototypical instance model:

When a test item or problem is presented, it is first coded, and this representation serves to activate stored instances from memory. The basis for access is the similarity of the test item and stored instances. One or more of the stored instances then serve as an analog for the test item. More specifically, a mapping is made between certain aspects of the retrieved instance and known aspects of the test item; this mapping then licenses the transfer of other aspects of the retrieved instance to unknown aspects of the test item. There are, therefore, three major stages: coding, access, and mapping.

This sketch of a model captures the general structure of current analogy models (e.g., Gentner, 1983; Holyoak, 1984; Holyoak and Thagard, 1989). In applying the sketch to the phenomenon captured by Criterion 1, two critical questions arise. The first is whether the representation of an instance coded the special structure of the rule, or is instead restricted to more concrete information. To illustrate, suppose you have stored an instance of the statement, "If you drive a motorcycle in Michigan, then you must be over 17"; the question of interest amounts to whether your stored instance includes information equivalent to *If p implies q; p; therefore q*. If an instance representation does include such information, then it essentially includes the rule. This strikes us not only as implausible, but also as contrary to the intended meaning of "instance." In particular, one does not think of an instance as containing variables. In what follows, then, we will assume that instances do not encode the abstraction they instantiate, though often they may encode features that are correlated with the abstraction. Thus, instance models differ from rule models not just in whether the test item accesses an instance or rule, but also in how abstractly the test item is coded to begin with. . . .

The second critical question for an instance model is how to compute the similarity between the test item and the stored instance. If the similarity is computed over all features, then the model cannot explain the phenomenon of equal accuracy for familiar and unfamiliar items, because there is no guarantee that the stored instances most similar to "gork implies flum" will be useful in dealing with the test item. Perhaps "glory and fame" will be retrieved, and this conjunction is of no use in dealing with the test item. . . .

To salvage an instance model we must assume that the similarity between the test item and stored instance is computed over very restricted features, namely, those correlated with the special structure of the rule. Consider again a stored instance of the regulation, "If you drive a motorcycle in Michigan, you must be over 17." The representation of this instance may well contain features corresponding to the concepts *if* and *then*, where these features are correlated with modus ponens. If such features were given great weight in the similarity calculation, a useful analog might be retrieved. There are, however, three problems with the assumption of differential weighting. First, it is ad hoc. Second, it may be wrong, as a growing body of evidence indicates that the retrieval of analogs is influenced more by concrete features, like appearance and taxonomic category, than abstract ones (e.g., Gentner and Toupin, 1986; Holyoak and Koh, 1987; Ross, 1987). Third, for some rules there may be no obvious features correlated with the rule's special structure (a good example is the law of large numbers, as we will see later). In short, when it comes to explaining the phenomenon that accuracy is as high for novel rule-based items as for familiar ones, an instance model seems to be either wrong or ad hoc. As we will see, the same conclusion holds for many of the other phenomena we consider [Smith, Langston, and Nisbett, 1992, pp. 8–10].

The Second Criterion of Rule Use

The second criterion and its rationale are presented in the following section.

Criterion 2: Performance with Rule-Governed Items is as Accurate with Abstract as with Concrete Materials.

Rationale. This criterion is similar to our first one. However, whereas Criterion 1 was concerned with unfamiliar or nonsensical items, Criterion 2 is concerned with abstract items that may in fact be very familiar. To appreciate Criterion 2, note that intuition suggests that the rule modus ponens can readily be applied to a totally abstract item, such as "If A then B; A; therefore B." (This item is abstract in the sense of containing few features, and possible, in the sense of containing variables.) Good performance on this item fits with the sketch of a rule model we presented earlier, because there is no reason to expect that abstract items are less likely than concrete ones to access the modus ponens rules, and no reason to expect abstract items to fare less well than concrete ones in instantiating the rule or inspecting an instantiated representation. If anything, we might expect abstract items to be both more likely to access a rule and easier to instantiate, because abstract items are more similar to the rule than are concrete items. Note further that good performance on abstract items is quite difficult to explain in terms of an instance model, because the only thing that an abstract item and a retrieved instance can possibly have in common is the special structure of the rule. That is, the use of abstract items allows one to strip away all content but the special structure, and consequently, performance must be based on the special structure alone (Rips, 1990). For these reasons, Criterion 2 is among the most diagnostic ones we will consider [Smith, Langston, and Nisbett, 1992, pp. 14–15].

The Third Criterion of Rule Use

The third criterion and its rationale are given in the following account.

Criterion 3: Early in Acquisition, a Rule May Be Applied to an Exception (a Rule Is Overextended).

Rationale. In psycholinguistics, this criterion has figured prominently in studies of how children master the regular past-tense form of English verbs. The relevant rule is to add "ed" to the stem of verbs to form the past tense, such as "cook-cooked." A finding that has been taken as evidence for following this rule is tendency of young children to overextend the rule to irregular forms, such as "go-goed," even though they had previously used the irregular form correctly (Ervin, 1964). The rule specifies a special structure—the stem of the verb—and the phenomenon arises because children apply the rule to items containing the special structure even though the items should have been marked as exceptions. In terms of our sketch of a model, early in acquisition, exceptional verbs are likely to be represented in a way that accesses the relevant rule, and once the rule is accessed it is instantiated and applied.

Perhaps for more than any other criterion, there has been a concerted effort to formulate non-rule-based accounts of overextension. Thus, Rumelhart and McClelland (1987) offered a connectionist account of the overextensions of classification rules (see, e.g., Medin and Smith, 1981). In general, then, this criterion seems less diagnostic than the previous two we considered. We include it, though, because it may prove to be diagnostic in specific cases. Indeed, with regard to overextension of the past-tense rule, critiques of the Rumelhart and McClelland proposal by Pinker and Prince (1988) and Marcus et al. (1990) suggest that a rule-based theory still provides the fullest account of the data. The critics noted, for example, that children are no more likely to overgeneralize an irregular verb that is similar to many regular ones than to overgeneralize an irregular verb that is similar to few regular ones. Yet, in most connectionist models, as in instance models, generalization is based on similarity. The lack of similarity effects fits perfectly with the rule-based account, of course. Thus, in situations where the likelihood of overgeneralizing an exception does not depend on the similarity of the exception to the regular cases, the criterion is indeed diagnostic [Smith, Langston, and Nisbett, 1992, pp. 16–17].

The Fourth Criterion of Rule Use

The fourth criterion and its rationale are presented in the following section.

Criterion 4: Performance on a Rule-Governed Problem Deteriorates as a Function of the Number of Rules that Are Required to Solve the Problem.

Rationale. Criterion 4 essentially holds that rules provide the appropriate unit for measuring the complexity of a problem. We can illustrate the criterion by considering problems that vary in the number of times they require application to the rule modus ponens. Even after equating for reading time, deciding that Argument 2 is valid presumably would take longer and be more error prone than deciding that Argument 1 is valid, because Argument 2 requires one more application of modus ponens:

1. If it's raining, I'll take an umbrella
   It's raining

   _____

   I'll take an umbrella

2. If it's raining , I'll take an umbrella
   If I take an umbrella , I'll lose it
   It's raining

   _____

   I'll lose an umbrella

(Our example might suggest that the phenomenon is an artifact of the premises being more complex in Argument 2 than in Argument 1; however, using correlational techniques, Rips [1983] found no evidence that premise complexity per se affects the accuracy of reasoning.)

The phenomenon of interest follows from our sketch of a rule model as long as one or more of the stages involved—coding, access, instantiation, and application—is executed less efficiently when it has to do $n + 1$ things than just n things. As many theorists have pointed out, this vulnerability to sheer number may disappear with extended practice. In Anderson's (1982) rule-based model of cognitive skills, for example, rules that are frequently applied in succession come to be "compiled" or chunked into a simple rule; in such a case, performance would be rule-based yet fail to meet Criterion 4. The diagnosticity of this criterion is further reduced by the fact that the basic phenomenon involved seems roughly compatible with an instance model: What needs to be assumed is that problems that supposedly require more rules are really just problems that generally have fewer or less accessible analogues in memory. Again, though, we include the criterion because it may prove very diagnostic in certain cases, for example, in cases where there is a *linear* relation between the number of rules that a problem requires and the reaction time needed to solve the problem. Also, the criterion has a history of use in evaluating rule-based hypotheses. For example, in psycholinguistics, it figured centrally in testing the hypothesis that the complexity of a sentence was an increasing function of the number of transformational rules needed to derive the surface form of the sentence (Miller, 1962) [Smith, Langston, and Nisbett, 1992, pp. 18–19].

The Fifth Criterion of Rule Use

The fifth criterion and its rationale are given in the following account.

Criterion 5: Performance on a Rule-Based Item Is Facilitated when Preceded by Another Item Based on the Same Rule (Application of a Rule Primes Its Subsequent Use).

Rationale. The rationale for this criterion is that, once used, a mental structure remains active for a brief time period and during this period the structure is more accessible than usual. In terms of our rule model, the access stage has been facilitated. (Anderson, 1982, made a similar assumption relating recency of rule use to ease of subsequent access.) Our sketch of an instance model would be able to account for the phenomenon to the extent that successively presented rule-based items are also similar in content) but as we will see, the plausibility of this account depends on the specific findings involved [Smith, Langston, and Nisbett, 1992, pp. 19–20].

The Sixth Criterion of Rule Use

The sixth criterion and its rationale are presented in the following section.

Criterion 6: A Verbal Protocol May Mention a Rule or Its Components.

Rationale. The rationale for this criterion is based on the standard interpretation of protocol analysis. Presumably, the protocol is a direct reflection of what is active in the subject's short-term or working memory (Ericsson and Simon, 1984), and if a particular rule has been in working memory, then it may have been recently used. Or, to put it in terms of our sketch of a rule model, the products of the access, instantiation, or application stages may reside (perhaps only briefly) in working memory, which makes then accessible to report. There is no reason to expect an instance model to yield such reports. However, the protocol criterion is still of limited diagnosticity, given that there are cases of apparent rule following in which the rules cannot be reported (namely, in language), as well as cases of reported rules for tasks for which there is independent evidence that the rules were not followed (Nisbett & Wilson, 1977) [Smith, Langston, and Nisbett, 1992, pp. 20–21].

The Seventh Criterion of Rule Use

The seventh criterion and its rationale are given in the following account.

Criterion 7: Performance on a Specific Rule-Based Problem Is Improved by Training on an Abstract Version of the Rule.

Rationale. The idea behind this criterion is that, because rule following is presumably what underlies performance on specific problems, practice on an abstract version of the rule (abstract in all senses we have considered) can improve performance on specific problems. In part, this could be true because training improves the rule—clarifies it, renders it more precise, and even changes its nature so as to make it more valid. From the perspective of our sketch of a rule model, practice on the rule in the abstract could also benefit performance by increasing the accessibility of the rule and perhaps also by facilitating the application of the rule. (To the extent that there were any examples in the training, there could be a facilitation of the instantiation stage as well.) From the perspective of an instance model, there is no obvious reason why such abstract training should have any effect on performance. Criterion 7 is therefore quite diagnostic [Smith, Langston, and Nisbett, 1992, p. 22].

The Eighth Criterion of Rule Use

The eighth criterion and its rationale are given in the following account.

Criterion 8: Performance on Problems in a Particular Domain Is Improved as Much by Training on Problems Outside the Domain as on Problems Within it, as Long as the Problems are Based on the Same Rule.

Rationale. If a major product of training is an abstract rule that is as applicable to problems from one domain as to those from another, then subjects taught how to use the rule in a given context domain should readily transfer what they have learned to other domains. To put it in terms of our sketch of a rule model: The major products of training are increased in the accessibility of the rule and in the consequent ease with which the rule can be instantiated and applied, and all of these benefits should readily transfer to domains other than those of the training problems. The upshot is that domain-specificity effects of training might be relatively slight. To the extent such effects are slight, instance models are embarrassed because they naturally predict better performance for test problems that resemble training ones. Hence, Criterion 8 is very diagnostic of rule following [Smith, Langston, and Nisbett, 1992, pp. 24–25].

Summary of Major Results

Smith, Langston, and Nisbett (1992) present the following summary of their major results.

Throughout most of this article we have been concerned with two interrelated matters: possible criteria for rule following and possible rules that are followed. Let us first summarize our progress regarding the possible criteria, then turn to what we have found out about rules.

Criteria. We have presented and defended a set of criteria for establishing whether or not a rule is used for solving a given problem. Satisfaction of the less diagnostic of these criteria—those concerned with overextension, number of rules, priming, and protocols—adds something to the case that a given rule is used for solving a given problem. Satisfaction of the more diagnostic criteria—those concerned with familiarity, abstractness, abstract training effects, and domain independence in training—adds even more to the case for rule following. And satisfaction of most or all of these criteria adds greatly to the case for rule following. These criteria can serve to put the debate between abstraction-based and instance-based reasoning into clearer perspective.

[Table 2.1] presents each of the eight criteria crossed with the five different rule systems we have examined in detail; broken lines indicate that the rule system failed the criterion of interest. [Table 2.1] makes it easy to see a pair of points concerning the criteria. One is that most of the criteria has been relatively haphazard, with many tests of a particular criterion for some rules and only one or two tests of a smattering of the other criteria. We suspect that the criteria used have been chosen relatively arbitrarily, and that investigators often have tested less powerful criteria than they might have, simply because they were not aware of the existence of the other, more powerful ones. Our overview of criteria and the rationales behind them should help to organize and direct research on the use of rules.

The other point about the criteria that is readily apparent from [Table 2.1] is that the criteria converge. That is, if a rule passes one criterion it generally passes any other criterion that has been applied. Conversely, if a rule fails one criterion it generally fails other criteria that have been applied. We have only one case of this convergence of failures—modus tollens—because our main concern has been with abstract rules that are likely to be in people's repertoires. If we turn our attention to unnatural rules, which are unlikely to be in people's repertoires, we should see other failures to satisfy the criteria. Consider, for example, work by Ross (1987), in which people were taught relatively unnatural rules from probability theory, such as the rule that specifies the expected number of trials to wait for a particular probabilistic event to occur (the "waiting time" rule). Ross

TABLE 2.1

Criteria for Use of Abstract Rules for Reasoning and Evidence Base Relating to Them.

Criteria	Rule Types				
	Modus Ponens	Modus Tollens	Contractual (Permissions & Obligations)	Causal	Law of Large Numbers
1. Good performance on unfamiliar items	Byrne (1989)	///////////// Cheng & Holyoak (1985) Numerous Others //// /////////////	Cheng et al. (1986) Cheng & Holyoak (1985)	Morris et al. (1991)	Nisbett et al (1983)
2. Good Performance on abstract items	Evans (1977)	Wason (1966) / / / / / Numerous Others / / / /	Cheng & Holyoak (1985)		
3. Overextension early in training					Fong et al. (1986)
4. Number of rules and performance	Osherson (1975) Rips (1983) Braine et al. (1984)				
5. Priming effects			Langston et al. (1991)		
6. Protocols identify rules	Rips (1983)	////			Piaget & Inhelder (1951/1975) Jepson et al. (1983) Nisbett et al. (1983) Fong et al. (1986)
7. Abstract training effects	///////////// Cheng et al. (1986) ///////////// ///////////// /////////////	///////////// Cheng et al. (1986) ///////////// ///////////// /////////////	Cheng et al (1986)	Morris, Cheng, & Nisbett (1991)	Fong et al. (1986) Lehman & Nisbett, (1990)
8. Domain independence of training					Lehman et al. (1988) Fong et al. (1986) Fong & Nisbett (1991)

Note: Broken lines indicate rule system filed the criterion of interest.
Source: Smith, Langston, and Nisbett, 1992, p. 28.

observed a strong violation of our domain-independence-of-training criterion; that is, performance on a test problem markedly depended on its similarity to a training problem. Recent results by Allen and Brooks (1991), who taught subjects artificial rules, make exactly the same point. These failures of unnatural rules to pass the criterion attest to the validity of the criteria.

Three qualifications of the criteria are also worth mentioning. First, for purposes of clarity we have stated some of our criteria in an absolute or all-or-none fashion, but probably it would be more useful to treat each criterion in a relative fashion. We can illustrate this point with Criterion 1, *performance on rule-governed items is as accurate with unfamiliar as familiar items.* Taking the criterion literally, there is evidence for rule-following only when there is absolutely *no* difference between unfamiliar and familiar items. But surely the phenomenon that underlies the criterion admits of degrees, perhaps because of moment-to-moment variations in whether an individual uses a rule. Given this, Criterion 1 is better stated as *the less the difference in performance between unfamiliar and familiar rule-governed items, the greater the use of rules.* Similar remarks apply to Criterion 2 (good performance on abstract items), Criterion 7 (abstract training effects), and Criterion 8 (domain independence of training). It is noteworthy that actual uses of theses criteria tend to employ the relative interpretation (see e.g., the Allen and Brooks, 1991, use of domain-independence-of-training effects).

A second qualification of the criteria stems from the fact that their diagnosticity has been measured in terms of how difficult they are to explain by models based on *stored* instances. But Johnson-Laird (1983) has championed a theoretical approach which holds that people reason by generating *novel* instances (in his terms, "reasoning by means of mental models"). To illustrate, suppose someone is told, "If gork then flum." They would represent this conditional in terms of the following sort of mental model:

gorkl = flum 1
gork2 = flum 2
        (flum 3).

The equal sign indicates that the same instance is involved, and the parentheses indicate that the instance is optional. If now told there exists a gork, one can use this mental model to conclude there also exists a flum, and in this way implement modus ponens. What is important about this for our purposes is that a theory based on such novel instances seems more compatible with our criteria than theories based on stored instances. For example, there is no obvious reason why one cannot construct a mental model as readily for an unfamiliar item as for a familiar one, or as readily for an abstract item as a concrete one.

The final qualification is simply that the application of our criteria does not provide as definitive data on the rule-versus-instance issue as does a contrast of detailed models. Our criteria are needed mainly in situations where detailed reasoning models have not yet been developed: the usual case as far as we can tell. (An exception is Nosofsky, Clark, and Shin, 1989, who did contrast detailed rule and instance models, but who considered rules that are not abstract by our definitions.) Our criteria also provide useful constraints in developing detailed rule models; for example, any rule model that is concerned only with abstract rules ought to produce comparable performance for unfamiliar and familiar items, for abstract and concrete items, and so on.

Rules. [Table 2.1] also tells us about what rules are followed. We believe that the applications of the criteria to data serve to establish that people make use of a number of abstract rules in solving problems of a sort that occur frequently in everyday life. In particular, there is substantial evidence for at least three sorts of rule systems.

For modus ponens, there is evidence that people: (a) perform as well—that is, make inferences in accordance with the rule—on unfamiliar as on familiar material; (b) perform as well on abstract as on concrete material; (c) perform better if they must invoke the rule fewer rather than more times; and (d) sometimes provide protocols suggesting that they have used the rule. (On the other hand, there is some evidence that the rule cannot be trained by abstract techniques, but this evidence may merely indicate that the rule is already asymptotic.)

For contractual rules, namely permission and obligation rules, there is evidence that people: (a) perform as well on unfamiliar as on familiar material; (b) perform as well on abstract as on concrete material; (c) show priming effects of the rule, at least within a content domain; and (d) benefit from training in their ability to apply the rule to any material that can plausibly be interpreted in terms of it. There is also some evidence of a comparable kind for formally similar causal rules.

For the system of statistical rules under the rubric of the law of large numbers, it has been shown that people: (a) perform well with unfamiliar material; (b) overextend the rule early in training; (c) often mention the rule in relatively abstract form in justification of their answers for particular problems; (d) improve in their ability to apply the rule across a wide number of domains by purely abstract training on the rule; and (e) improve their performance on problems outside the domain of training as much as on problems within it.

The demonstrations that people follow modus ponens and the law of large numbers are of particular interest in view of the fact that these two rules are normative and promote optimal inferential performance. Evidence for people following certain abstract inferential rules thus amounts to evidence for people manifesting aspects of rationality. Although there is less data about causal rules, what evidence there is suggests that people also follow these rules (see [Table 2.1]), which again are normative. And there is some recent evidence for the use of still another set of normative rules, those governing economic choices (Larrick et al., 1990).

In contrast to the positive evidence summarized before, there are three lines of negative evidence on the question of whether people use modus tollens. It has been shown that people perform poorly: (a) with unfamiliar items; (b) with abstract items; and (c) even after formal training in the rule. We therefore believe that the consensus among students of the problem that most people do not use modus tollens is justified in terms of the criteria studied to date. This demonstration indicates that application of our criteria can cut both ways: Negative evidence relating to the criteria can cast substantial doubt on the use of a rule, just as positive evidence can buttress the case for its use.

Of course modus ponens, modus tollens, contractual rules, and the law of large numbers are just a handful of the many possible seemingly natural rules that people may follow in reasoning about everyday problems. There are, for example, numerous rules in propositional logic other than ponens and tollens that have been proposed as psychologically real (see, for instance, Braine et al., 1984). One such rule is *and-introduction,* which states *if p is the case and if q is the case then p and q is the case.* The obvious question is: How does and-introduction stack up against our eight criteria? The same question applies to other rules from propositional logic, and to rules that have figured in Piagetian-type research (including transitivity, commutativity, and associativity), as well as to rules that come from other bodies of work. The point is that all we have done in this article is sample a rule or two from a few major branches of reasoning—deduction, statistics, and causality—and there are other rules of interest in these and other branches of reasoning.

A final point to note about the evidence for rules is that the work to date shows not merely that people *can* follow rules when instructed to do so in artificial problem-solving situations, but that they *do* follow quite abstract inferential rules when solving ordinary, everyday problems. For example, in their studies of the law of large numbers, Fong et al. (1986) performed not merely laboratory experiments, but field studies in which subjects did not even know they were being tested. In one study, male subjects were called in the context of an alleged "survey on sports opinions." Subjects were enrolled in introductory statistics courses and were called either at the beginning or at the end. After being asked a few questions about NBA salaries and NCAA rules, it was pointed out to them that although many batters often finish the first two weeks of the baseball season with averages of .450 or higher, no one has ever finished the season with such an average. They were asked why they thought this was the case. Most subjects responded with causal hypotheses such as, "the pitchers make the necessary adjustments." Some, however, responded with statistical answers such as, "there are not many at-bats in two weeks, so unusually high (or low) averages would be more likely; over the long haul nobody is really that good." There were twice as many statistical answers from subjects tested at the end of the term as from subjects tested at the beginning.

Similarly, Larrick et al. (1990) found that subjects who were taught cost-benefit rules came to apply them in all sorts of life contexts, from consumer decisions about whether to finish a bad meal or a bad movie, to professional decisions about whether to pursue a line of work that was turning out to be disappointing, to hypothetical questions about institutional policy and international relations.

Thus, the work reviewed here establishes not merely that people can follow abstract rules self-consciously in appropriate educational, experimental, or professional settings, but that such rules play at least a limited role in ordinary inference [Smith, Langston, and Nisbett, 1992, pp. 26–32].

Abstract Models and Instance Models

Smith, Langston, and Nisbett (1992) discuss the issue of abstract models and instance models in the following section.

Combining Rule and Instance Mechanisms

Our review indicates that pure instance models of reasoning and problem solving are not viable. There is too much evidence, stemming from the application of too many criteria, indicating that people use abstract rules in reasoning. On the other hand, there is also abundant evidence that reasoning and problem solving often proceed via the retrieval of instances (e.g., Allen and Brooks, 1991; Kaiser, Jonides, and Alexander, 1986; Medin and Ross, 1989; Ross, 1987). At a minimum, then, we need to posit two qualitatively different mechanisms of reasoning. Whereas some situations may involve only one of the mechanisms, others may involve both.

In addition to *pure-rule* and *pure-instance* mechanisms, hybrid mechanisms may be needed as well. In particular, hybrid mechanisms may be needed to account for the situations noted earlier in which people process instances deeply enough to encode some information about the relevant abstraction as well as about the concrete aspects of the instance. These are the situations that are the concern of most case-based reasoning models (e.g., Hammond et al., 1991; Kolodner, 1983; Schank, 1982). In such situations, people have essentially encoded both an instance and a rule, so a hybrid mechanism must specify how the two representational aspects are connected. We consider two possibilities.

One possibility is that a retrieved instance provides access to a rule. That is, when an item is presented, it first accesses similar instances from memory that the reasoner can use to access a rule. Then, the final stages of rule processing—instantiation and application—ensue, though the instance may serve as a guide for these two stages. We can illustrate this mechanism with the drinking version for the four-card problem. When presented the problem, presumably a subject uses this item to retrieve from memory an episode of a drinking event; this representation may contain the information that people below the drinking age are in violation of the law, and the concept of *violation* may be used to access the permission rule; from here on, processing would continue as specified in our sketch of a rule model except that the retrieved instance can be used to guide the instantiation and application stages. This hybrid process, which we will refer to as *instance-rule mechanism*, captures the intuition that we often understand an abstract rule in terms of a specific example.

The other possibility is that a rule provides access to a relevant instance (a *rule-instance* mechanism). That is, when an item is presented it is coded abstractly, and this abstraction accesses the appropriate rule (these are the first two stages of our sketch of a rule model). The rule then provides access to some typical examples, and these instances control further processing. Again, we can illustrate with the drinking version of the four-card problem. When presented the problem, a subject codes the item in terms of *permission*, and uses this code to access the permission rules. Associated with these rules are typical examples of *permission* situations, and one or more of these instances is used as an analog for the present problem (that is, it is used for the mapping stage).

A few comments are in order about these mechanisms. Note that we are not proposing the two hybrid mechanisms as alternatives to the two pure mechanisms (rule and instance). Rather, we suspect that all four mechanisms can be used, albeit with different situations recruiting different mechanisms. (The experimental situations we reviewed in this article likely involved either the *pure-rule* or the *pure-instance* mechanism.) In situations where more than one mechanism is involved, presumably the processes operate simultaneously and independently of one another. Thus, the final answer may be determined by a kind of "horse race" between the operative mechanisms, with the mechanism that finishes first determining the final judgment.

Note further that our hybrid mechanisms allow room for instance-type effects should they occur. Consider again Criterion 1, that novel rule-based items are treated as accurately as familiar ones. The available evidence is consistent with this criterion, but the criterion deals only with accuracy. Perhaps if one were to measure reaction times, familiar rule-based items might be processed faster than novel ones. Such a result could be handled easily by our *instance-rule* mechanism. Familiar items should be faster in accessing a relevant instance because familiar items are themselves likely to be instances. In addition, we have already seen the indication of instance effects even for accuracy. Such an effect appeared in connection with Criterion 5, that application of a rule primes its subsequent use. Recall that in the four-card problem, Langston et al. (1991) found evidence for priming of contractual rules only when the prime and target were similar in content. This pattern of results also fits nicely with the *instance-rule* mechanism. Only when the target and prime are similar in content does the target retrieve the prime instance, and only when the prime is retrieved does one gain access to the relevant rule. Thus, instance-type effects do not imply that rules were not involved.

Finally, another case of instance-type effects during rule use is provided by Ross (1987). Ross trained subjects on the waiting-time rule of probability theory and then had them solve new test problems with the rule present. Even though the rule was present, subjects appeared to rely on training problems when determining how to instantiate the rule. These results indicate that instances are used not just to access a rule but also to help instantiate it, as in the instance rule mechanism. (These results, however, may depend in part on the fact that the rule involved was not a natural one.)

In short, the dichotomy between pure rules and pure instances is too simple. Hybrid mechanisms seem plausible, particularly in light of the role they play in current versions of case-based reasoning [Smith, Langston, and Nisbett, 1992, pp. 32–34].

Types of Rule Following

Smith, Langston, and Nisbett (1992) discuss the issue of types of rule following in the following section.

Two Kinds of Rule Following

Until now we have acted as if explicit rule following is the only kind of rule following. But a critical observation suggests the need to consider a second kind. The observation (due to Douglas Medin, personal communication, April 1991) is that, when *linguistic* rules are stacked up against our eight criteria they seem to consistently fail three of them, namely verbal protocols, abstract training effects, and context independence in training. That is, people are notoriously unable to verbalize the linguistic rules they purportedly use, and they fail to benefit much from explicit (school) instructions on these rules. If linguistic rules meet only five of our criteria whereas reasoning rules (generally) meet all eight, perhaps the kind of rule following involved in language is different from that involved in reasoning.

Presumably there is a kind of rule following that is *implicit* rather than *explicit*; that is, the rule is never explicitly represented, which accounts for why it can neither be reported nor affected by explicit instruction. The rule might be implemented in the hardware, and is essentially a description of how some built-in processor works (see Pinker and Prince, 1988, Section 8.2). Implicit rules are close to what we earlier characterized as operating principles of a system, and rules like this may be part of our basic cognitive architecture. Such notions fit nicely with Pylyshyn's (1984) concept of *cognitive penetrability*. His basic idea is that anything that is part of the fixed cognitive architecture cannot be altered (penetrated) by goals, context, or instruction. If some linguistic rules are part of our basic architecture, they should not be affected by instruction, which means that our two instructional criteria should fail, as they in fact do (The seeming imperviousness of modus ponens to instruction leaves open the possibility that this rule too may be represented implicitly) [Smith, Langston, and Nisbett, 1992, p. 34].

Connectionist Models and Rule Use

Smith, Langston, and Nisbett (1992) analyze the meaning of their results with respect to the doctrine of connectionism, in the following section.

Implications for Connectionist Models

Although we know of no limit, in principle, on the ability of connectionist models to code abstractions, the evidence we have presented for abstract rules does not fit well with the connectionist program.

For one thing, what seems to be the most straightforward account of much of the evidence involves concepts that are anathema to connectionism. The account we have in mind is that of explicit rule following: The rule and input are mentally represented explicitly, and application of the rule to the input involves an inspection of the input to determine whether the antecedent of the rule has been satisfied. Notions of *explicit data structures* and *inspection of explicit structures* simply lie outside the ontology of connectionism. Of course, connectionists may be able to develop alternative accounts of the data, but there is no reason to believe the resulting connectionist models will be as parsimonious as the sort of rule-based model we advocate. This is particularly the case given that the abstract rules that have to be modeled all involve variable bindings, which remains a difficult issue in connectionist work (for discussion, see Holyoak, 1991). In short, rule-based models provide a simple account of the data, and no comparable connectionist alternatives are thus far in sight.

In constructing alternative models of the evidence, connectionists face another difficulty. The evidence indicates that people can use two qualitatively different mechanisms in reasoning, which we have termed "rules" and "instances," whereas connectionist models can either blur the rule-instance distinction, in which case they are simply failing to capture a major generalization about human cognition, or they can somehow mark the distinction, in which case they may be merely implementing a rule-based model in a connectionist net. We say "merely" because it is not clear that such an implementation will yield any new important insights about reasoning.

The preceding points have been programmatic, but the remaining one is more substantive. According to rule models, the rationale for some rules hinges on a *constituency relation*—like that which holds between *If p then q* and *p*—but most current connectionist models lack true constituency relations. In discussing this issue, we need to keep separate *localist* connectionist models, in which a concept can be represented by a single node, and *distributed* models, in which a concept is represented by a set of nodes. We consider localist models first.

To understand the constituency issue, consider modus ponens. Given *If p then q* and *p*, the fact that the latter is a constituent of the former is part of why we can conclude *q*. To take an even simpler example, consider again and-introduction: *If p is the case and if q is the case then p and q is the case.* Here, it is clear that the basis of the rule is a constituency relation; the rule essentially states, *if each of its constituents is the case, then a conjunction is the case.* In contrast, localist connectionist models lack constituency relations, so such relations can never serve as the basis for rules.

The reason localist connectionist models lack constituency relations is that their nodes (their representations) lack any internal structure, including a part-whole structure. In a localist model for and-introduction, for example, there might be separate nodes for p, q, and p and q, which are connected in such a way that whenever the nodes for p and q are both activated, the node for p and q has no internal structure, and in no sense contains the node for p or that for q. Hence, the relation between the p and q nodes on the one hand, and the p and q node on the other, is strictly causal (as opposed to constituency). That is, activation of p and q causes activation of p and q in exactly the same way that activation of *fire* might cause activation of a node for *smoke*. Although we know of no data on whether constituency relations are perceived as the bases of some rules, our intuitions suggest they are, which favors the rule account. (For a fuller discussion of these issues, see Fodor and Pylyshyn, 1988.)

Distributed connectionist models seem better able to accommodate constituency relations because they at least have a part-whole structure. Thus, if p and q is represented by a set of nodes, then some part of that set can, in principle, represent p and another part q. However, current distributed connectionist models still have trouble capturing constituent structure, as Fodor and McLaughlin (1990) pointed out. The latter authors take up a proposal by Smolensky (1988), in which a concept (rule) is represented in terms of a vector whose components represent the activity levels of the members of the relevant set of nodes. According to Smolensky, vector a is a constituent of vector b if there exists a third vector—call it x—such that $a + x = b$; a is a part of b because b is derivable from $a(+ x)$. But this proposal permits the possibility that b may be activated without a being activated. In the case of and-introduction, this means that p and q could be activated without p being activated. Such a thing should be impossible if p is a true constituent of p and q. Again, to the extent some rules are based on constituent structure, the rule account is favored over current connectionist rivals.

None of this is to suggest that connectionist models do not have an important role to play—they have been very successful in capturing aspects of perception, memory, and categorization, for example—but rather to suggest that some aspects of reasoning may be inherently rule-based, and hence, not naturally captured by connectionist models. Of course, a rule-based model, unlike a connectionist one, will not look like a biological model. Thus, to pursue rule-based models of reasoning is to give up the wish that all mental phenomena be expressive of biological phenomena rather than merely neural connections to abstract rules that seem metaphorically to sit astride the hustle and bustle of biological activity in the brain, altering and managing the results of such activity, and being modified by the mere world of outsiders and the ministrations of educators. We do not pretend to be able to make the leap from the known facts of the behavior of the nervous system to a plausible, emergent set of highly modifiable abstract rules. We claim merely that a correct theory of mind may have to do so [Smith, Langston, and Nisbett, 1992, pp. 34–37].

Commentary

A fourfold classification can be imposed on mechanisms in reasoning: pure rule-based, pure instance-based, hybrid rule-instance-based, and hybrid instance-rule-based. The class of rule-based mechanisms is mapped in the research of Smith, Langston, and Nisbett (1992). Their methodology with suitable adaptations should be applied to the other three classes, resulting in summary tables analogous to Table 2.1. The resulting set of summary tables would constitute a descriptive classification.

The next strategic research advance would move from a descriptive classification to a dynamic analysis focused on the simultaneity and interaction of the mechanisms that operate in extended reasoning and problem-solving tasks. This empirical analysis should be placed under the theoretical aegis of a hybrid symbolic-connectionist architecture.

3

The Generality of Creative Mechanisms in Intelligent Reasoning

Scientific Discovery and Artificial Intelligence

The General Logic of BACON.3

The process of scientific discovery depends on the detection of patterns in data and the summary representation of these patterns in theoretical terms. BACON.3 uses general heuristics and production system methodology to accomplish pattern detection and the discovery of scientific laws. Among the classical laws rediscovered by BACON.3 is Kepler's third law of planetary motion. It must be emphasized that BACON.3's discoveries of scientific laws do not entail an explanation of the data; the laws only provide a summary of the data in the form of equations. In this section, BACON.3, developed by Langley (1981), will be described with respect to its major characteristics. An example of the system's behavior will be provided, a summary and analysis of BACON.3's discoveries will be presented, and a commentary on BACON.3's strengths and limitations will be offered.

Characteristics of BACON.3

To discover scientific laws, BACON.3 relies on a set of general heuristics that recast data and theoretical terms at increasingly abstract levels of description. The first set of these heuristics operates at the level of data collection. The functions of these data-gathering productions are summarized in Section 1 of Table 3.1.

To recast the collected data, BACON.3 applies a set of heuristics that discern patterns or regularities and lead to higher levels of description. A summary of productions that detect regularities is given in Section 2 of Table 3.1.

A third set of heuristics is devoted to the calculation of the values of theoretical terms at a given level of description. The process of calculating theoretical values is summarized in Section 3 of Table 3.1.

A fourth set of productions is devoted to the detection of redundancies of new theoretical terms with existing theoretical terms. This process of redundancy detection is summarized in Section 4 of Table 3.1.

A fifth set of productions controls an abstraction process whereby differences in theoretical terms can be ignored. This process of ignoring differences and creating abstractions at higher levels of description is summarized in Section 5 of Table 3.1.

A sixth set of productions is devoted to the process of combining clusters that have identical conditions. This process of collapsing clusters with identical conditions into single structures is summarized in Section 6 of Table 3.1.

A seventh set of productions is directed toward the detection of irrelevant variables and to dropping their values from consideration. The mechanisms for discovering irrelevant variables and controlling their effects are summarized in Section 7 of Table 3.1.

The BACON.3 system depends on these seven sets of productions (86 productions in all) for the discovery of physical laws. The following subsection contains an example of BACON.3's discovery process: the discovery of a version of Kepler's third law of planetary motion.

BACON.3's Discovery of Kepler's Third Law

The general methodology of BACON.3, as discussed previously and summarized in Table 3.1, was applied in the discovery of physical laws originally discovered by Kepler, Galileo, Ohm, and others. In the following account of an interesting approach to the rediscovery of Kepler's third law, material in brackets identifies the general set of heuristics (Table 3.1) used in various stages of the discovery process (Langley, 1981, pp. 40–42).

> Kepler's third law relates a planet's distance from the sun to its period of revolution. The law also holds for other bodies with satellites, such as Jupiter, though the constant involved is different. The law may be stated as $d^3/p^2=c$, where d is the distance from the central body, p is the period,

TABLE 3.1

Set of productions in the BACON.3 system.

___

1. Gathering Data

    The first set of 17 productions is responsible for gathering directly observable data. Of these productions, 7 are responsible for gathering information from the user about the task to be considered. This information consists of the names of all variables, along with suggested values for those variables under the system's control. Once this information has been gathered, the remaining 10 productions gather data through a standard factorial design.

    First the values of one independent term are varied while those of the others are held constant. Next, the value of the second variable is incremented and all values of the first are again considered under these conditions. This continues until all values of the second term have been generated. Now the value of the third variable is incremented, and the cycle begins again. In this manner, all combinations of independent variable values are eventually generated. The values of all dependent variables are observed for each combination.

2. Discovering Regularities

    The second set of 16 productions is responsible for noting regularities in the data collected by the first set. These rules can temporarily interrupt the data gathering productions while pursuing their own goals. The system's regularity detectors can be divided into a set of <u>constancy detectors</u> and a set of <u>trend detectors</u>. The first of these can deal with either symbolic or numerical data; they create higher level descriptive clusters by formulating generalizations and finding the conditions on them. BACON.3's trend detectors operate only on numerical data.

3. Calculating Theoretical Values

    Once a theoretical term has been defined at a given level, 3 additional productions calculate the values of this term for the clusters at that level. Since a theoretical term is tied to a particular level of description, the values of some terms are obtained only after considerable work has been done at lower levels. Once these values have

___

Source: Langley, P. (1981). Data-Driven Discovery of Physical Laws. <u>Cognitive Science</u>, <u>5</u>, 31 - 54. Reprinted with the permission of the Ablex Publishing Corporation.

TABLE 3.1, continued

Set of productions in the BACON.3 system.

---

been calculated, they are fair game for the regularity detectors and new levels of description may be created and more complex theoretical terms may be defined. This results from the fact that defined terms are not distinguished from directly observable variables when noting regularities.

4. Noting Redundant Theoretical Terms

Before calculating the values of a new theoretical term, BACON.3 must make sure that the term is not equivalent to an existing concept. If a redundant term's values were calculated, then mathematically valid but empirically uninteresting relationships (e.g., $x/x = 1$) could be detected. Accordingly, a fourth set of 22 productions decomposes new terms into their primitive components. If the definition of a new variable is identical to an existing definition, the term is rejected and other relations are considered (or, in the case of a linear relationship, the new term is replaced by the old).

5. Ignoring Differences

Suppose BACON.3 has defined two intercept concepts,.... The values of the first, $intercept_{pv,t,1}$ are 0 when the number of moles is 1, while the values of a second, $intercept_{pv,t,2}$ are 0 when the number of moles is 2. One would like BACON.3 to generalize at this point, stating that the intercept of all lines relating the pressure · volume to the temperature is 0, regardless of the number of moles. However, because the two intercepts are different terms, the constancy detector described above cannot be applied.

BACON.3's solution to this problem is to note the definitions of the two intercepts differ only by a constant coefficient, and to define an abstraction of the two which ignores this difference. Abstracted terms are tied to one level higher than the terms from which they are created; there is no need to rediscover a constancy that is already known, so the abstracted values are copied directly to the higher level clusters. Once these values have been copied, the regularity detectors can be applied, in this case, the value of the abstracted term is always 0.

Source: Langley, P. (1981). Data-Driven Discovery of Physical Laws. Cognitive Science, 5, 31 - 54. Reprinted with the permission of the Ablex Publishing Corporation.

TABLE 3.1, continued

Set of productions in the BACON.3 system.

---

6. Collapsing Clusters

When a constancy is noted, a higher level description is created and conditions are found for it. Later, if a constancy is observed on a different variable, a separate cluster is specified. If the two clusters have identical conditions, they are combined into a single structure; only 3 productions are devoted to this process. Once this has happened to a number of cluster pairs, the values of the dependent terms can be compared and regularities may emerge.

For example, suppose BACON.3 has run experiments with a pendulum at various locations and found that Galileo's pendulum law, $P^2/L=K$, holds at each location. In this equation, P is the period of the pendulum and L is the length of the support. However, suppose the value of K varies at each location. Now, imagine that BACON.3 drops a set of objects at each location, and finds that the acceleration of these objects also differs according to the location. Upon combining the information acquired at identical locations, a regularity is detected. Since the acceleration increases as the period²/length increases, the product acceleration · period²/length is considered; the value of this term is constant regardless of the location.

7. Handling Irrelevant Variables

Consider again Galileo's law for pendulums, and assume BACON.3 begins by varying the values for four independent variables--length of the support, the location of the experiment, the weight of the supported object, and the initial angle of the support with respect to the vertical. In fact, both the weight and the angle (if small values are examined) are irrelevant to the period of the pendulum, but this is not obvious from the outset.

To deal with such situations, BACON.3 draws on a set of 8 productions. The most important of these nodes clusters is the level in which the description for a variables value is two more than the level at which the variable was defined; this implies that the variable most recently varied has had no effect on the dependent values. The effect of this production is to modify the data gathering scheme so the value

---

Source: Langley, P. (1981). Data-Driven Discovery of Physical Laws. Cognitive Science, 5, 31 - 54. Reprinted with the permission of the Ablex Publishing Corporation.

TABLE 3.1, continued

Set of productions in the BACON.3 system.

---

considered is used for the rest of the run. The remaining productions carry out the details of this process.

8. Summary of the Discovery Method

In summary, BACON.3 gathers data in systematic fashion, varying one term at a time and observing its effects. If a variable has no effects, it is marked as irrelevant and its manipulation is abandoned. If one variable does influence another, a new theoretical term is defined, incorporating both the independent and the dependent variables. If this term has not been considered before, its values are computed and examined. When these values are constant, BACON.3 creates a new, higher level description which it treats as data on that level. The new cluster may be combined with others if it has identical conditions. When the values of the new term are not constant, it is used to define a more complex term and the process repeats. In addition, the search for useful theoretical terms and constancies occurs anew at each level of description. Taken together, these heuristics make BACON.3 a powerful yet general discovery system.

Source: Langley, P. (1981). Data-Driven Discovery of Physical Laws. Cognitive Science, 5, 31 - 54. Reprinted with the permission of the Ablex Publishing Corporation.

and c is a constant. The levels of description approach suggest an interesting way to discover this law. Assume a simplified solar system in which all orbits are circular. This has two important implications. First, the distance between a satellite and the body it orbits is a constant over time. Second, it implies that equal fractions of a satellite's orbit are covered in equal times. This second point can be derived from Kepler's second law, that equal areas of an orbit are covered in equal times.

BACON.3 is given control [Section 1 of Table 3.1] over three observational variables—an origin object, a vector object, and the time at which this pair of objects are observed. Two dependent variables [Section 1 of Table 3.1] are used. One of these is the distance between the observed origin and vector objects. The second assumes a fixed coordinate such as a star, which is distant enough that motions within the solar system can be effectively ignored in computing angles with respect to it. (This is true of even the closest stars. Astronomers attempted to use the method of parallax to estimate stellar distances for over a century before their instruments were made sensitive enough to detect any motion.) BACON.3 is given access to the angle made using a fixed star and vector object as the end points, and using the origin object as the pivot point.

BACON.3 begins by collecting [Section 1 of Table 3.1] values of these last two attributes for various pairs of solar objects at various times. [Table 3.2] shows some of the data gathered in this manner. The program quickly discovers [Section 2 of Table 3.1] that in some cases certain values of the distance recur. The conditions found [Section 2 of Table 3.1] for the resulting generalizations are that the origin object is one of the planets. A set of second-level descriptions are created [Section 2 of Table 3.1], describing these regularities.

Concurrently, BACON.3 notices [Section 2 of Table 3.1] that as the time increases, the angles seem to increase. (This assumes knowledge that this variable's values are cyclical—e.g., that $30° - 90° = 300°$.) In each case, the slope of the angle with respect to the time is a different constant. As a result, theoretical terms for the slopes and intercepts of these linear relations are defined [Section 2 of Table 3.1], with slightly different concepts being created to describe different lines. The conditions under which these relations hold are also found [Section 2 of Table 3.1]. The resulting clusters are presented in [Table 3.3].

Next, BACON.3 notices [Section 6 of Table 3.1] that it has a number of second-level clusters with identical sets of conditions, but with different generalizations. Accordingly, it collapses [Section 6 of Table 3.1] these clusters and places slopes, intercepts and distances together. The next step in finding Kepler's third law is to relate the distances to the slope of the angles with respect to time. However, each slope is a different theoretical term, and in this form they cannot be compared with the distances.

First, BACON.3 must realize that each of these concepts' definitions differ only by a single numerical parameter, and that since it has just moved up a level of description, it might ignore [Section 5 of Table 3.1] these differences and treat these terms as identical. The parameters are no longer needed since the values of the slopes have already been calculated, so the program creates [Section 5 of Table 3.1] a new, more abstract variable for the slope of the angle with respect to the time, and replaces the old terms with this new one. A similar process is applied to the intercepts.

Now BACON.3 has second-level data it can examine, and immediately finds [Section 2 of Table 3.1] a monotonic decreasing relation between the distance d and the slope s. A new variable, ds, is defined [Section 2 of Table 3.1] and its value examined; now the system notes [Section 2 of Table 3.1] a decreasing relation between ds and the distance. Another term is created [Section 2 of Table 3.1]; d^2s and ds also seem inversely related, so their product, d^3s^2 is defined as a new variable. This term is found to have a constant value, so a third-level descriptive cluster is generated [Section 2 of Table 3.1]; in each case, the Sun is the origin object, so this is added [Section 2 of Table 3.1] as a condition to the rule.

Later, when BACON.3 considers a different set of objects, Jupiter and its satel l ites, these variables stand it in good stead. Rather than having to repeat the process, it simply calculates [Section 3 of Table 3.1] the values of existing concepts. Again the theoretical term d^3s^2 is found [Section 2 of Table 3.1] to be constant, but this time with a different value. The common aspect of these clusters is that Jupiter is the origin object, so this is added

TABLE 3.2

First-Level Data of the Solar System.

Origin	Vector	Time	Distance	Angle	Slope A,T
Sun	Mercury	50	0.38719	52.909	4.09090
Sun	Mercury	60	0.38719	52.909	4.09090
Sun	Mercury	70	0.38719	52.909	4.09090
Sun	Venus	50	0.72398	49.000	1.60000
Sun	Venus	60	0.72398	65.000	1.60000
Sun	Venus	70	0.72398	81.000	1.60000
Sun	Earth	50	1.00000	185.860	0.98563
Sun	Earth	60	1.00000	195.710	0.98563
Sun	Earth	70	1.00000	205.570	0.98563

Source: Langley, P. (1981). Data-Driven Discovery of Physical Laws. Cognitive Science, 5, 31 - 54. Reprinted with the permission of the Ablex Publishing Corporation.

TABLE 3.3

Second-Level Description of the Solar System.

Origin	Vector	Distance	Slope A,T	DS	D²S	D³S²
Sun	Mercury	0.38719	4.090900	1.58400	0.61330	0.97146
Sun	Venus	0.72398	1.600000	1.15840	0.83864	0.97146
Sun	Earth	1.00000	0.985630	0.98563	0.98563	0.97146
Sun	Mars	1.52370	0.544020	0.79847	1.21670	0.97146
Sun	Jupiter	5.19910	0.083141	0.43226	2.24740	0.97146
Sun	Saturn	9.53850	0.033457	0.31913	3.04410	0.97146

Source: Langley, P. (1981) Data-Driven Discovery of Physical Laws. *Cognitive Science*, 5, 31-54. Reprinted with the permission of the Ablex Publishing Corporation.

[Section 2 of Table 3.1] as a condition to this new third-level descriptive cluster. Note that the values of s are inversely proportional to the planet's periods, so that $d^3 s^2 = .97146$ is an alternate formulation of Kepler's third law [Langley, 1981, pp. 407–42].

Scientific Discoveries of BACON.3

In addition to the discovery of a version of Kepler's third law, BACON.3 discovered a number of other empirical laws. In this section, the empirical laws, their diversity, and their relative complexity will be discussed. The generality of BACON.3's methodology will be considered in two ways: (1) the extent to which each of its seven sets of heuristics (Table 3.1) was involved in the discoveries; and (2) the effect of changing the order of the experiments that lead to the discoveries.

BACON.3 discovered five scientific laws: the ideal gas laws, Kepler's third law, Coulomb's law, Galileo's laws, and Ohm's law. The equations for these laws are presented in Table 3.4.

In the equation for the ideal gas laws, n is the quantity of gas (in moles), p is the pressure exerted in the gas, V is the volume of the gas, T is the temperature of the gas (in degrees Kelvin) and K_1 is a constant.

TABLE 3.4

Equations Discovered by BACON.3

Ideal gas law	$pV/nT = K_1$
Kepler's third law	$d^3[(a-k_2)/t]^2 = k_3$
Coulomb's law	$Fd^2/q_1 q_2 = k_4$
Galileo's laws	$dP^2/Lt^2 = k_5$
Ohm's law	$D^2T/(LI + k_6 D^2 I) = k_7$

Source: Langley, P. (1981) Data-Driven Discovery of Physical Laws. Cognitive Science, 5, 31-54. Reprinted with the permission of the ABLEX Publishing Corporation.

In the equation for Kepler's third law, the expression in brackets is the slope of the angle with respect to time (as described in the previous section), d is the distance of the planet (or satellite) from the Sun (or central body), and k_3 is a constant (.97146, as described in the previous section).

In the equation for Coulomb's law, F is the electrical force between two spheres (in a torsion balance), d is the initial distance between the two spheres, q_1 and q_2 are charges on the spheres, and k_4 is a constant (8.99×10^9 Newton-meters^2 / Coulombs^2).

In the equation for Galileo's laws (the law of pendulum motion and the law of uniform acceleration), P is the period of the pendulum, L is the length of the support, d is the distance traversed after an object is dropped, t is the elapsed time after the object was dropped, and k_5 is a constant.

In the equation for Ohm's law, T is the temperature differential at the ends of a metal bar to which the ends of a copper wire are tapped, L is the length of the wire, D is the diameter of the wire, I is the current through the wire, and k_6 and k_7 are constants.

The empirical laws discovered by BACON.3 exhibit diversity in subject matter and in algebraic expression: from the laws of the solar system to the physics of motion, gases, and electricity; from the squaring of a ratio (Kepler's law) to simple ratios and products (ideal gas laws) to the ratio of squared variables (Galileo's laws).

The algebraic complexity of Ohm's law suggests computational complexity in its discovery. As compared with the other laws, the discovery of Ohm's law required a larger number of productions, a larger size of working memory, more levels of description, and more theoretical terms.

BACON.3's heuristics appear to be general across the set of five empirical laws. This generality held in the case of five sets of productions: factorial experimental design in the collection of data (Section 1 of Table 3.1), discovering the regularities (Section 2 of Table 3.1), calculating theoretical values (Section 3 of Table 3.1), noting redundant theoretical terms (Section 4 of Table 3.1), and collapsing clusters (Section 6 of Table 3.1). The heuristics involved in the development of abstractions by ignoring differences (Section 5 of Table 3.1) was used in the discovery of four of the laws (the discovery of Galileo's laws was the exception). The productions involved in the handling of irrelevant variables (Section 7 of Table 3.1) were used only for the discovery of Galileo's laws.

The generality of the BACON.3 system is indicated by its ability to arrive at the empirical laws by various orders or sequences of experimental observations. Variations in order could lengthen or shorten the time required to discover a law, but the identical law was still discovered. Computational complexity (e.g., number of productions used, size of working memory) was an experimental order effect, but the attainment of the empirical law was not an experimental order effect.

Commentary on BACON.3

BACON.3 embodies a set of heuristics that perform, in machine fashion, intellective functions of induction, abstraction, generalization, factorial experimentation, and calculation. The machine executes these intellective functions under the guidance of its symbolic language.

The heuristic codes are, as indicated in the previous section, general in the sense that they can execute different content, but the heuristic codes are indifferent to and uncomprehending of the content. The comprehension lies with the human user of BACON.3. BACON.3 did not independently discover or rediscover any laws; it merely executed heuristic codes, designed and interpreted by its developer.

BACON.3 produced equations that are descriptive and empirical. Its heuristics can no doubt be extended to other descriptive laws in physics and other domains (Langley, Simon, Bradshaw, and Zytkow, 1987). However, its heuristics are inadequate for theoretical conceptualization of the complex explanatory laws that constitute contemporary knowledge in such areas as nuclear physics.

In conclusion, BACON.3 is a machine representation of the inductive and Baconian (Francis Bacon, 1561–1626), method of descriptive science. It remains to be seen whether artificial intelligence research (Caudill and Butler, 1990; Partridge and Wilkes, 1990) can develop machine representation (Kulkarni and Simon, 1988) of discovery in theoretical science (Wagman, 1991, Chapter 4).

The Generality of Analogical Mapping in Intelligent Reasoning

Analogical Mapping in the ACME System

The Nature of Analogical Thinking

Thinking is sometimes deductive, sometimes inductive, and sometimes analogical. Deductive thinking has the character of formal logical representations and derivations; inductive thinking looks to the accumulated balance of positive and negative instances; analogical thinking seeks correspondences between the features of two sets of concepts or objects. Analogical thought can serve the purpose of setting forth an explanation of correspondence of elements in known situations with those in fully understood situations. Scientific discovery processes are often aided by analogical thought. In political, economic, and intellectual movements analogies are widely used in argumentation and persuasion. Analogies in the form of expressive metaphors and similes are prevalent in classical literature and everyday language.

A theory of analogical thinking and a computational model of the theory has been developed by Holyoak and Thagard (1989). Their interesting research will be described and the implications of their theory and model will be discussed in a commentary section.

The General Logic of Analogical Mapping by Constraint Satisfaction

The general logic of analogical mapping requires a set of criteria or constraints that delimit the essential correspondences or similitudes between two analogs, typically a source analog and a target analog. Three delimiting and interacting constraints are stipulated in the theory advanced by Holyoak and Thagard (1989):

> *The structural constraint of isomorphism* encourages mappings that maximize the consistency of relational correspondences between the elements of the two analogs.
> *The constraint of semantic similarity* supports mapping hypotheses to the degree that mapped predicates have similar meanings.
> *The constraint of pragmatic centrality* favors mappings involving elements the analogist believes to be important in order to achieve the purpose for which the analogy is being used [p. 295, italics added].

The ACME Model of Analogical Mapping

Holyoak and Thagard (1989) developed ACME, a cooperative algorithm for analogical mapping that is directed toward the satisfaction of the sets of interactive constraints described in the previous section. The rationale for the use of a cooperative algorithm in analogical mapping is set forth in the following assertions.

> Several properties of an information-processing task can provide cues that a cooperative algorithm may be appropriate. A cooperative algorithm for parallel constraint satisfaction is preferable to any serial decision procedure when: (a) a global decision is composed of a number of constituent decisions, (b) each constituent decision should be based upon multiple constraints, (c) the outcome of the global decision could vary depending upon the order in which constraints are applied and constituent decisions are made, and (d) there is no principled justification for preferring a particular order of constraints or of constituent decisions. Analogical mapping using constraints exhibits all of these features [Holyoak and Thagard, 1989, pp. 306–307].

ACME (Analogical Constraint Mapping Engine), as a parallel architecture, constructs a network of nodes or units that represent hypotheses and produces an optimal mapping as an outcome of program processing. There are a number of general features in the design of ACME's network, its nodes, and hypotheses bearing out the relationship between the source analog and the target analog.

Each possible hypothesis about a possible pairing of an element from the source with a corresponding element of a target is assigned to a node or *unit*. Each unit has an *activation level,* ranging between some minimum and maximum values, which indicates the plausibility of a corresponding hypothesis, with higher activation indicating greater plausibility. Inferential Dependencies between mapping hypotheses are represented by *weights* or *links* between units. Supporting evidence is given a negative weight. . . . The input to the program consists of predicate-calculus representations of the source and target analogs, plus optional information about semantic similarity and pragmatic importance. It is assumed that a mapping may be computed either from a target analog to a source or vice versa. It is conjectured that the direction of the mapping will vary depending upon the use of the analogy and the knowledge of the analogist. If the source is much more familiar than the target, then it may be best to try to map source elements to target elements. On the other hand, if the source is much more complicated than the target or if the target contains highly salient elements, then the analogist may attempt to map from the target to the source. . . . When given two structures as input, ACME automatically generates a network in accord with the constraints postulated by the theory. . . . As units are established, links are formed between them to implement the constraint of structural consistency. All links are symmetrical, with the same weight regardless of direction. . . . In addition to the units representing mapping hypotheses, the network includes two special units. The *semantic unit* is used to convey information about the system's prior assessment of the degree of semantic similarity between each pair of meaningful concepts in the target and source, and the *pragmatic unit* similarly is used to convey information about the pragmatic importance of possible correspondences. The semantic-similarity constraint is enforced by placing excitatory links from the semantic unit to all units representing mappings between predicates. The weights of these links are made proportional to the degree of semantic similarity between the mapped concepts. Similarly, the pragmatic-centrality constraint is represented by weights on links connecting the pragmatic unit to relevant mapping units [Holyoak and Thagard, 1989, pp. 308–312].

General Applications of ACME

As the implementation of a general theory of analogical thinking, ACME should be able to apply its analogical mapping functions to analogical problem solving, analogical argumentation, analogical explanation, and analogical metaphor.

Major contexts for analogy use include problem solving, when the solution to one problem suggests a solution to a similar one; argumentation, when similarities between two situations are used to contend that what is true in one situation is likely to be true in the other; and explanation, when a familiar topic is used to provide understanding of a less familiar one. In addition, analogical reasoning is also used to understand formal analogies of the sort found in mathematics, as well as metaphors, which can be employed to serve both explanatory and more aesthetic functions [Holyoak and Thagard, 1989, p. 318].

It is impressive that ACME does, in fact, apply its mapping algorithms to the many various contexts in which analogical reasoning takes place. Table 4.1 summarizes the types of analogies mapped by ACME and some network characteristics of each mapping.

ACME's analogical reasoning ability can be appreciated by considering two extremes in its range of applications. These are ACME's ability to process formal mathematical analogies on the one hand and literary metaphors on the other hand.

Application of ACME to a Formal Mathematical Analogy

ACME was applied to the problem of discovering a formal analogy between two mathematical concepts: the addition of numbers and the union of sets. The analogy is formal in that it depends only on isomorphic or structural constraints and is devoid of semantic and pragmatic content.

[Table 4.2] presents a formal analogy between addition of numbers and union of sets. . . . Both addition and union have the abstract mathematical properties of commutativity, associativity, and the existence of an identity element (0 for numbers and ∅ for sets). ACME was given predicate-calculus representations of these two analogs, with no identical elements (note that number equality and set equality are given distinct symbols), and with all semantic weights set equal to the minimal value. This analogy is quite complex, as many propositions have the same predicates (sum or union), and many symbols representing intermediate results must be sorted out. Note that the representations given to the program did not explicitly group the components of each analog into three distinct equations. In the absence of any semantic or pragmatic information, only weights based upon isomorphism, coupled with the type restriction, provided information about the optimal mapping.

As the output in [Table 4.3] indicates, ACME settles to a complete solution to this formal mapping problem after 59 cycles. The model is thus able to derive a unique mapping in the absence of any overlap between the elements of the source and target. ACME's ability to deal with such examples is crucially dependent upon its parallel constraint-satisfaction algorithm [Holyoak and Thagard, 1989, pp. 340–341].

TABLE 4.1

Summary of Applications of ACME.

Analogs	Number of Units	Number of Symmetric Links
Lightbulb/radiation problems (4 versions) (Holyoak & Koh, 1987)	169-192	1373-1773
Fortress/radiation problems (Gick & Holyoak, 1980)	41	144
Cannibals and missionaries/farmer's dilemma problems (Gholson et al., 1986)	144	973
Contras interference	95	169
Politics interference (2 versions)	55-67	308-381
Water-flow/heat-flow explanation (2 versions) (Falkenhainer et al., 1986)	62-127	317-1010
Solar system/atom explanation (Falkenhainer et al., 1986)	93	733
Jealous animal stories (6 versions) (Gentner & Toupin, 1986)	125-214	1048-1873
Addition/union	162	1468
Attribute mapping	43	220
Midwife/Socrates (3 versions) (Kittay, 1987)	97-203	534-1702
Chemical analogies (8 different analogies) (Thagard et al., 1989)		

Source: Holyoak, K.J., & Thagard, P. (1989). Analogical Mapping by Constraint Satisfaction. Cognitive Science, 13, 295-355. Reprinted with the permission of the Ablex Publishing Corporation.

TABLE 4.2

Formal Isomorphism Between Addition of Numbers and Union of Sets.

Property	Addition	Union
Commutativity:	N1 + N2 = N2 + N1	S1 ∪ S2 = S2 ∪ S1
Associativity:	N3 + (N4 + N5) =	S3 ∪ [S4 ∪ S5] =
	(N3 + N4) + N5	[S3 ∪ S4] ∪ S5
Identity:	N6 + 0 = N6	S6 ∪ ∅ = S6

Predicate-Calculus Representations:

NUMBERS:

(sum (num1 num2 num10) n1)
(sum (num2 num1 num11) n2)
(num_eq (num10 num11) n3)
(sum (num5 num6 num12) n3)
(sum (num4 num12 num13) n5)
(sum (num4 num5 num14) n6)
(sum (num14 num6 num15) n7)
(num_eq (num13 num15) n8)
(sum (num20 zero num20) n9)

SETS:

(union (set1 set2 set10) s1)
(union (set2 set1 set11) s2)
(set_eq (set10 set11) s3)
(union (set5 set6 set12) s4)
(union (set4 set12 set13) s5)
(union (set4 set5 set14) s6)
(union (set14 set6 set15) s7)
(set_eq (set13 set15) s8)
(union (set20 empty-set set20) s9)

Source: Holyoak, K.J., & Thagard, P. (1989). Analogical Mapping by Constraint Satisfaction. Cognitive Science, 13, 295-355. Reprinted with the permission of the Ablex Publishing Corporation.

TABLE 4.3

Output after Running Addition/Union Analogy.

Network has settled by cycle 59.

Test: TEST0 Total Times: 60

Mon May 2 10:40:03 EDT 1988

Analogy between numbers and sets.

Units not yet reached asymptote: 0

Goodness of network: 3.31

Calculating the best mappings after 60 cycles.

Best mapping of NUM10 is SET 10. 0.79

Best mapping of NUM2 is SET 2. 0.82

Best mapping of NUM1 is SET 1. 0.82

Best mapping of NUM11 is SET 11. 0.79

Best mapping of NUM12 is SET 12. 0.82

Best mapping of NUM6 is SET 6. 0.82

Best mapping of NUM5 is SET 5. 0.82

Best mapping of NUM13 is SET 13. 0.79

Best mapping of NUM4 is SET 4. 0.82

Best mapping of NUM14 is SET 14. 0.82

Best mapping of NUM15 is SET 15. 0.79

Best mapping of NUM20 is SET 20. 0.66

Best mapping of ZERO is EMPTY-SET. 0.66

Best mapping of NUM_EQ is SET_EQ. 0.57

Best mapping of SUM is UNION. 0.83

Source: Holyoak, K.J., & Thagard, P. (1989). Analogical Mapping by Constraint
Satisfaction. Cognitive Science, 13, 295-355. Reprinted with the
permission of the Ablex Publishing Corporation.

Application of ACME to a Literary Metaphor

ACME's ability to map metaphors was tested by confronting it with two versions of a classical metaphor in which Socrates is the midwife of an idea. The correct version is the straightforward metaphor, but in the incorrect version misleading and confusing information is introduced. In the following account, the correct version is referred to as the isomorphic version.

> The run reported in the first column of [Table 4.4] used the isomorphic version without any pragmatic weights. The network settles with a correct set of mappings after 34 cycles. Thus Socrates maps to the midwife, his student to the mother, the student's intellectual partner to the father, and the idea to the child. (Note that there is a homomorphic mapping of the predicates thinks_about and tests_truth to in_labor_with.) The propositions analogs are not essential here; deletion of them still allows a complete mapping to be discovered [Holyoak and Thagard, 1989, p. 344].

In the nonisomporphic version or incorrect version, ACME's performance in mapping the metaphor is potentially degraded by the introduction of inappropriate data.

> The nonisomorphic version contains the information that Socrates drinks hemlock juice, which is of course irrelevant to the metaphor. Far worse, the representation encodes the information that Socrates himself was matched to his wife by a midwife; and that Socrates' wife had a child with the help of this midwife. Clearly, this nonisomorphic extension will cause the structural and semantic constraints on mapping to support a much more superficial set of correspondences between the two situations. And indeed, in this second run, ACME finds only the barest fragments of the intended metaphoric mappings when the network settles after 105 cycles. Socrates' midwife now maps to the midwife in the source, and Socrates' wife and child map to the source mother and child. Socrates himself simply maps to the father. Most of the other crucial objects and predicates (other than cause and helps, which map to themselves) have no good mappings. The only major pieces of the intended analogy that survive are the mappings between the student and the mother and between the idea and the child.
>
> Note, however, that the original statement of the metaphor, "Socrates is a midwife of ideas," provides some direct pragmatic guidance as to the intended mappings. Clearly, Socrates must map to the midwife, and the idea must map to something. This is precisely the kind of knowledge that ACME can represent using pragmatic weights. Accordingly, in a further run the mappings between propositions sl and ml and between the elements of those propositions (i.e., sl=ml, Socrates=obj_midwife, and philosopher=midwife) were marked as PRESUMED; and proposition s4 and its elements (i.e., s4, obj_idea, and idea) were marked as IMPORTANT. The right column on [Table 4.1] reports the results for the nonisomorphic

TABLE 4.4

Best Mappings, with Asymptotic Activation Levels, for Objects and Predicates in Three Versions of the Socrates/Midwife Metaphor.

	Versions					
Cycles to Settle	Isomorphic Nonpragmatic 34		Nonisomorphic Nonpragmatic 105		Nonisomorphic Pragmatic 83	
Objects:						
Socrates	obj_midwife	.87	obj_father	.80	obj_midwife	.86
obj_student	obj_mother	.69	obj_mother	.69	obj_mother	.69
obj_partner	obj_father	.81	none		obj_father	.80
obj_idea	obj_child	.90	obj_child	.69	obj_child	.70
*obj_soc-midwife	--		obj_midwife	.84	none	
*obj_soc-wife	--		obj_mother	.69	obj_mother	.69
*obj_soc-child	--		obj_child	.69	obj_child	.65
*obj_hemlock	--		none		none	
Predicates:						
philospher	midwife	.58	none		midwife	.81
student	mother	.59	none		none	
intellectual_partner	father	.57	none		father	.57
idea	child	.59	none		child	.58
introduces	matches	.77	none		matches	.67
formulates	conceives	.72	conceives	.27	conceives	.31
thinks_about	in_labor_with	.36	none		none	
tests_truth	in_labor_with	.36	none		none	
knows_truth_or_falsify	gives_birth_to	.72	gives_birth_to	.72	gives_birth_to	.72
helps	helps	.77	helps	.79	helps	.80
cause	cause	.84	cause	.84	cause	.84
*poison	--		none		none	
*drink	--		none		none	
*father	--		father	.70	none	
*midwife	--		midwife	.70	none	
*mother	--		mother	.69	mother	.69
*child	--		child	.69	none	
*matches	--		matches	.78	none	
*conceives	--		conceives	.48	conceives	.43
*in_labor_with	--		in_labor_with	.74	in_labor_with	.74
*gives_birth_to	--		gives_birth_to	.46	gives_birth_to	.43

* Elements with an asterisk appeared only in nonisomorphic version. Elements that map to "none" have no mapping unit with activation greater than 20.

Source: Holyoak, K.J., & Thagard, P. (1989). Analogical Mapping by Constraint Satisfaction. Cognitive Science, 13, 295-355. Reprinted with the permission of the Ablex Publishing Corporation.

version of the metaphor after these pragmatic weights are introduced. The pragmatic information was sufficient to allow almost complete recovery of the abstract metaphoric mappings. The network settled after 83 cycles. Socrates again maps to the midwife, and the partner to the father; almost all of the appropriate predicate mappings, such as those between idea and child and between introduces and conceives, are also recovered. Note that some of the more superficial mappings of objects, such as between Socrates' wife and the mother, also emerge. *The behavior of the program across these versions of the metaphor thus dramatically illustrates both the power and the limitations of purely structural constraints, and the crucial role of pragmatic knowledge in finding abstract mappings in the face of misleading information* [Holyoak and Thagard, 1989, pp. 344–47, italics added].

Commentary

ACME's mapping performance is algorithmic and therefore it is not surprising that it should fall short of the flexibility and power found in human analogical reasoning. For example, ACME cannot handle the significant reasoning operation of the propositional converses. Thus, ACME is unable to map the converse relation between the inscribed proposition and the circumscribed proposition in plane and solid geometry.

ACME, as a computational approach to the generation and comprehension of analogies and metaphors, needs to be provided with vast amounts of knowledge that would enable it to be useful in complex human exposition of concepts, facts, and allusions. This knowledge requirement can be clearly seen in the following account of metaphor and theories of psychotherapy:

A metaphoric analysis of psychotherapy . . . contributes an understanding that is immediate, holistic, and idiographic. Psychoanalysis has a literary, classical, and dramatic metaphor (e.g., the incestuous conflicts of Oedipus, the obsessional struggles of Hamlet). Behavior therapy has a physiological, physicalistic, and mechanistic metaphor (e.g., deconditioning of anxiety responses, systematic training in adaptive behavior). Client-centered therapy has a personalistic, individualistic, and ideational metaphor (e.g., a search for self-identity, the discovery of personal values). Cognitive therapy has a rationalistic, logical, and educative metaphor (e.g., multiple and flexible rather than single and rigid interpretations of the meaning of life events, quality of cognition as precursor to quality of feeling). . . . These metaphors have the advantage of quickly capturing distinctive qualities in systems of psychotherapy [Wagman, 1988, p. 12].

5

The Generality of Explanatory Coherence in Intelligent Reasoning

The Theory of Explanatory Coherence and the Echo System

The Theory of Explanatory Coherence: Overview

Thagard (1989) has developed an important theory of intelligent explanatory reasoning. The theory of explanatory coherence has been implemented in the ECHO system. Thagard presents a summary of his theory and his research program in the following account.

This target article presents a new computational theory of explanatory coherence that applies to the acceptance and rejection of scientific hypotheses as well as to reasoning in everyday life. The theory consists of seven principles that establish relations of local coherence between a hypothesis and other propositions. A hypothesis coheres with propositions that it explains, or that explain it, or that participate with it in explaining other propositions, or that offer analogous explanations. Propositions are incoherent with each other if they are contradictory. Propositions that describe the results of observation have a degree of acceptability of their own. An explanatory hypothesis is accepted if it coheres better overall than its competitors. The power of the seven principles is shown by their implementation in a connectionist program called ECHO, which treats hypothesis evaluation as a constraint satisfaction problem. Inputs about the explanatory relations are used to create a network of units representing propositions, while coherence and incoherence relations are encoded by excitatory and inhibitory links. *ECHO provides an algorithm for smoothly integrating theory evaluation based on considerations of explanatory breadth, simplicity, and analogy. It has been applied to such important scientific cases as Lavoisier's argument for oxygen aqainst the phlogiston theory and Darwin's argument for evolution against creationism, and also to cases of legal reasoning.* The theory of explanatory coherence has implications for artificial intelligence, psychology, and philosophy [Thagard, 1989, p. 435].

The Theory of Explanatory Coherence: Principles

Thagard states the basic principles of the theory of explanatory coherence in the following terms.

I now propose seven principles that establish relations of explanatory coherence and make possible an assessment of the global coherence of an explanatory system S. S consists of propositions P, Q, $P_1 \ldots P_n$. Local coherence is a relation between two propositions. I coin the term "incohere" to mean more than just that two propositions do not cohere: To incohere is to *resist* holding together. The principles are as follows:

Principle 1. Symmetry
  (a) If P and Q cohere, then Q and P cohere.
  (b) If P and Q incohere, then Q and P incohere.

Principle 2. Explanation
  If $P_1 \ldots P_m$ explain Q, then:
  (a) For each P_i in $P_1...P_m$, P_i and Q cohere.
  (b) For each P_i and and P_j in $P_1...P_m$, P_j and P_i cohere.
  (c) In (a) and (b), the degree of coherence is inversely proportional to the number of propositions $P_1 \ldots P_m$.

Principle 3. Analogy
  (a) If P_1 explains Q_1, P_2 explains Q_2, P_1 is analogous to P_2, and Q_1 is analogous to Q_2, then P_1 and P_2 cohere, and Q_1 and Q_2 cohere.
  (b) If P_1 explains Q_1, P_2 explains Q_2, Q_1 is analogous to Q_2 but P_1 is disanalogous to P_2, then P_1 and P_2 incohere.

Principle 4. Data Priority
  Propositions that describe the results of observation have a degree of acceptability on their own.

Principle 5. Contradiction
  If P contradicts Q, then P and Q incohere.

Principle 6. Acceptability
  (a) The acceptability of a proposition P in a system S depends on its coherence with the proposition in S.
  (b) If many results of relevant experimental observations are unexplained, then the acceptability of a proposition P that explains only a few of them is reduced.

Principle 7. System Coherence
  The global explanatory coherence of a system S of propositions is a

function of the pairwise local coherence of those propositions [Thagard, 1989, pp. 436–437].

Thagard discusses the previous seven principles of explanatory coherence theory in the following account.

Principle 1, Symmetry, asserts that pairwise coherence and incoherence are symmetric relations, in keeping with the everyday sense of coherence as holding together. The coherence of two propositions is thus very different from the nonsymmetric relations of entailment and conditional probability. Typically, P entails Q without Q entailing P, and the conditional probability of P given Q is different from the probability of Q given P. But if P and Q hold together, so do Q and P. The use of symmetrical relation has advantages that will become clearer in the discussion of the connectionist implementation below.

Principle 2, Explanation, is by far the most important for assessing explanatory coherence, because it establishes most of the coherence relations. Part (a) is the most obvious: If a hypothesis P is part of the explanation of a piece of evidence Q, then P and Q cohere. Moreover, if a hypothesis P_2 is explained by another hypothesis P_1, then P_1 and P_2 cohere. Part (a) presupposes that explanation is a more restrictive relation than deductive implication, because otherwise we could prove that any two propositions cohere; unless we use relevance logic (Anderson and Belnap, 1975), P_1 and the contradiction P_2 & not-P_2 imply any Q, so it would follow that P_1 coheres with Q. *It follows from Principle 2(a), in conjunction with Principle 6, that the more a hypothesis explains, the more coherent and hence acceptable it is. Thus, this principle subsumes the criterion of explanatory breadth (which Whewell, 1967, called "consilience") that I have elsewhere claimed to be the most important for selecting the best explanation (Thagard, 1978; 1988a).*

Whereas part (a) of Principle 2 says that what explains coheres with what is explained, part (b) states that 2 propositions cohere if together they provide an explanation. Behind part (b) is the Duhem-Quine idea that the evaluation of a hypothesis depends partly on the other hypotheses with which it furnishes explanations (Duhem, 1954; Quine, 1961; . . .). I call two hypotheses that are used together in an explanation "cohypotheses." Again I assume that explanation is more restrictive than implication; otherwise it would follow that any proposition that explained something was coherent with every other proposition, because if P_1 implies Q, then so does P_1 & P_2. But any scientist who maintained at a conference that the theory of general relativity and today's baseball scores together explain the motion of planets would be laughed off the podium. Principle 2 is intended to apply to explanations and hypotheses actually proposed by scientists.

Part (c) of Principle 2 embodies the claim that if numerous propositions are needed to furnish explanation, then the coherence of the explaining propositions with each other and with what is explained is thereby diminished. Scientists tend to be skeptical of hypotheses that require myriad *ad hoc* assumptions in their explanations. There is nothing wrong in principle in having explanations that draw on many assumptions, but we should prefer theories that generate explanations using a unified core of hypotheses. I have elsewhere contended that the notion of *simplicity* most appropriate for scientific theory choice is a comparative one preferring theories that make fewer special assumptions (Thagard, 1978; 1988a). Principles 2(b) and 2(c) together subsume this criterion. I shall not attempt further to characterize "degree of coherence" here, but the connectionist algorithm described below provides a natural interpretation. Many other notions of simplicity have been proposed (e.g., Foster and Martin, 1986; Harman et al., 1988), but none is so directly relevant to considerations of explanatory coherence as the one embodied in Principle 2.

The third criterion for the best explanation in my earlier account was analogy, and this is subsumed in Principle 3. There is controversy about whether analogy is of more heuristic use, but scientists such as Darwin have used analogies to defend their theories; his argument for evolution by natural selection is analyzed below. Principle 3(a) does not say simply that any two analogous propositions cohere. There must be an explanatory analogy, with two analogous propositions occurring in explanations of two other propositions that are analogous to each other. Recent computational models of analogical mapping and retrieval show how such correspondences can be noticed (Holyoak and Thagard, 1989; Thagard et al., 1989). Principle 3(b) says that when similar phenomena are explained by dissimilar hypotheses, the hypotheses incohere. Although the use of such disanalogies is not as common as the use of analogies, it was important in the reasoning that led Einstein (1952) to the special theory of relativity: He was bothered by asymmetries in the way Maxwell's electrodynamics treated the case of (1) a magnet in motion and a conductor at rest quite differently from the case of (2) a magnet at rest and a conductor in motion.

Principle 4, Data Priority, stands much in need of elucidation and defense. In saying that a proposition describing the results of observation has a degree of acceptability on its own, I am not suggesting that is indubitable, but only that it can stand on its own more successfully than can a hypothesis whose sole justification is what it explains. A proposition Q may have some independent acceptability and still end up not accepted, if it is only coherent with propositions that are themselves not acceptable.

From the point of view of explanatory coherence alone, we should not take propositions based on observation as independently acceptable without any explanatory relations to other propositions. As Bonjour (1985) argues, the coherence of such propositions is of a nonexplanatory kind, based on background knowledge that observations of certain sorts are very likely to be true. From past experience, we know that our observations are very likely to be true, so we should believe them unless there is substantial reason not to. Similarly, at a very different level, we have some confidence in the reliability of descriptions of experimental results in carefully refereed scientific journals. . . .

Principle 5, Contradiction, is straightforward. By "contradictory" here I mean not just syntactic contradictions like P & not-P, but also semantic contradictions such as "This ball is black all over" and "This ball is white all over." In scientific cases, contradiction becomes important when incompatible hypotheses compete to explain the same evidence. Not all competing hypotheses incohere, however, because many phenomena have multiple causes. For example, explanations of why someone has certain medical symptoms may involve hypotheses that the patient has various diseases, and it is possible that more than one disease is present. Competing hypotheses incohere if they are contradictory or if they are framed as offering *the* most likely cause of a phenomenon. In the latter case, we get a kind of pragmatic contradictoriness: Two hypotheses may not be syntactically or semantically contradictory, yet scientists will view them as contradictory because of background beliefs suggesting that only one of the hypotheses is acceptable. For example, in the debate over dinosaur extinction (Thagard, 1988b), scientists generally treat as contradictory the following hypotheses:

(1) Dinosaurs became extinct because of a meteorite collision.
(2) Dinosaurs became extinct because the sea level fell.

Logically, (1) and (2) could both be true, but scientists treat them as conflicting explanations, possibly because there are no explanatory relations between them and their conjunction is unlikely.

The relation "cohere" is not transitive. If P_1 and P_2 together explain Q, while P_1 and P_3 together explain not-Q, then P_1 coheres with both Q and not-Q, which incohere. Such cases do occur in science. Let P_1 be the gas law that volume is proportional to temperature, P_2 a proposition describing the drop in temperature of a particular sample of gas, P_3 a proposition describing the rise in temperature of the sample, and Q a proposition about increases in the sample's volume. Then P_1 and P_2 together explain a decrease in the volume, while P_1 and P_3 explain the increase.

Principle 6, Acceptability, proposes in part (a) that we can make sense of the overall coherence of a proposition in an explanatory system just from the pairwise coherence relations established by Principles 1–5. If we have a hypothesis P that coheres with evidence Q by virtue of explaining it, but incoheres with another contradictory hypothesis, should we accept P? To decide, we cannot merely count the number of propositions with which P coheres and incoheres, because the acceptability of P depends in part on the acceptability of those propositions themselves. We need a dynamic and parallel method of deriving general coherence from particular coherence relations; such a method is provided by the connectionist program described below.

Principle 6(b), reducing the acceptability of a hypothesis when much of the relevant evidence is unexplained by any hypothesis, is intended to handle cases where the best available hypothesis is still not very good, in that it accounts for only a fraction of the available evidence. Consider, for example, a theory in economics that could explain the stock market crashes of 1929 and 1987 but that had nothing to say about myriad other similar economic events. Even if the theory gave the best available account of the two crashes, we would not be willing to elevate it to an accepted part of general economic theory. What does "relevant" mean here? [See BBS multiple book review of Sperber and Wilson's *Relevance,* BBS 10(4) 1987.] As a first approximation, we can say that a piece of evidence is *directly* relevant to a hypothesis if the evidence is explained by it or by one of its competitors. We can then add that piece of evidence is relevant if it is directly relevant or if it is similar to evidence that is relevant, where similarity is a matter of dealing with phenomena of the same kind. Thus, a theory of the business cycle that applies to the stock market crashes of 1929 and 1987 should also have something to say about nineteenth-century crashes and major business downturns in the twentieth century.

The final principle, System Coherence, proposes that we can have some global measure of the coherence of a whole system of propositions. Principles 1–5 imply that, other things being equal, a system S will tend to have more global coherence than another if

(1) S has more data in it;

(2) S has more internal explanatory links between propositions that cohere because of explanations and analogies, and;

(3) S succeeds in separating coherent subsystems of propositions from conflicting subsystems.

The connectionist algorithm described below comes with a natural measure of global system coherence. It also indicates how different priorities can be given to the different principles [Thagard, 1989, pp. 437–438, italics added].

ECHO: Input Formulas

The principles of explanatory coherence are represented in the connectionist program ECHO. In the following section, Thagard describes the input formulas to ECHO.

Let us now look at ECHO, a computer program written in Common LISP that is a straightforward application of connectionist algorithms to the problem of explanatory coherence. In ECHO, propositions representing hypotheses and results of observations are represented by units. Whenever Principles 1–5 state that two propositions cohere, an excitatory link between them is established. If two propositions incohere, an inhibitory link between them is established. In ECHO, these links are symmetric, as Principle 1 suggests: The weight from unit 1 to unit 2 is the same as the weight from unit 2 to unit 1. Principle 2(c) says that the larger the number of propositions used in an explanation, the smaller the degree of coherence between each pair of propositions. ECHO therefore counts the number of propositions that do the explaining and number proportionately lowers the weight of the excitatory links between units representing coherent propositions. . . .

The following are some examples of the LISP formulas that constitute ECHO's inputs (I omit LISP quote symbols; see [Tables 1–4] for actual input):

1. (EXPLAIN (H1 H2) E1)
2. (EXPLAIN (H1 H2 H3) E2)
3. (ANALOGOUS (H5 H6) (E5 E6))
4. (DATA (E1 E2 E5 E6))
5. (CONTRADICT H1 H4)

Formula 1 says that hypotheses H1 and H2 together explain evidence E1. As suggested by the second principle of explanatory coherence proposed above, formula 1 sets up three excitatory links, between units representing H1 and E1, H2 and E1, and H1 and H2. Formula 2 sets up six such links, between each of the hypotheses and the evidence, and between each pair of hypotheses, but the weight on the links will be less than those established by formula 1, because there are more cohypotheses. In accord with Principle 3(a), Analogy, formula 3 produces excitatory links between H5 and H6, and between E5 and E6, if previous input has established that H5 explains E5 and H6 explains E6. Formula 4 is used to apply Principle 4, Data Priority, setting up explanation-independent excitatory links to each data unit from a special evidence unit. Finally, formula 5 sets up an inhibitory link between contradictory hypotheses H1 and H4, as prescribed by Principle 5. A full specification of ECHO's inputs and algorithms is provided in the Appendix [Thagard, 1989, pp. 439–440].

ECHO: General Characteristics

In the following section Thagard summarizes the chief characteristics and capabilities of ECHO.

Program runs show that the networks thus established have numerous desirable properties. *Other things being equal, activation accrues to units corresponding by hypotheses that explain more, provide simpler explanations, and are analogous to other explanatory hypotheses.* The considerations of explanatory breadth, simplicity, and analogy are smoothly integrated. The networks are holistic, in that the activation of every unit can potentially have an effect on every other unit linked to it by a path, however lengthy. Nevertheless, the activation of a unit is directly affected by only those units to which it is linked. Although complexes of coherent propositions are evaluated together, different hypotheses in a complex can finish with different activations, depending on their particular coherence relations. The symmetry of excitatory links means that the active units tend to bring up the activation of units with which they are linked, whereas units whose activation sinks below 0 tend to bring down the activation of units to which they are linked. Data units are given priority, but can nevertheless be deactivated if they are linked to units that become deactivated. So long as excitation is not set too high . . . , the networks set up by ECHO are stable: In most of them, all units reach asymptotic activation levels after fewer than 100 cycles of updating. The most complex network implemented so far, comparing the explanatory power of Copernicus's heliocentric theory with Ptolemy's geocentric one, requires about 210 cycles before its more than 150 units have all settled [Thagard, 1989, p. 440; italics added].

ECHO: Applications To Scientific Explanatory Reasoning

ECHO has been applied to the comparative evaluation of competing scientific explanations as described by Thagard in the following section.

> To show the historical application of the theory of explanatory coherence, I shall discuss two important cases of arguments concerning the best explanation: Lavoisier's argument for his oxygen theory against the phlogiston theory, and Darwin's argument for evolution by natural selection. ECHO has been applied to the following:
> Contemporary debates about why the dinosaurs became extinct (Thagard, 1988b);
> Arguments by Wegener and his critics for and against continental drift (Thagard and Nowak 1988, in press);
> Psychological experiments on how beginning students learn physics (Ranney and Thagard 1988); and
> Copernicus's case against Ptolemaic astronomy (Nowak and Thagard, forthcoming) [Thagard, 1989, p. 444].

ECHO Applied to the Scientific Explanatory Reasoning of Lavoisier

In the following section Thagard presents an interesting account of how the competing phlogiston and oxygen theories were evaluated by ECHO.

> In the middle of the eighteenth century, the dominant theory in chemistry was the phlogiston theory of Stahl, which provided explanations of important phenomena of combustion, respiration, and calcination (what we would call oxidation). According to the phlogiston theory, combustion takes place when phlogiston in burning bodies is given off. In the 1770's, Lavoisier developed the alternative theory that combustion takes place when burning bodies combine with oxygen from the air (for an outline of the conceptual development of his theory, see Thagard, in press). More than ten years after he first suspected the inadequacy of the phlogiston theory, Lavoisier mounted a full-blown attack on it in a paper called "Reflexions sur le Phlogistique" (Lavoisier, 1862).

[Tables 5.1 and 5.2] present the input given to ECHO to represent Lavoisier's argument in his 1783 polemic against phlogiston. [Table 5.1] shows the 8 propositions used to represent the evidence to be explained and the 12 used to represent the competing theories. The evidence concerns different properties of combustion and calcination, while there are two sets of hypotheses representing the oxygen and phlogiston theories, respectively. . . .

[Table 5.2] shows the part of the input that sets up the network used to make a judgement of explanatory coherence. The "explain" statements are based directly on Lavoisier's assertions about what is explained by the phlogiston theory and the oxygen theory. The "contradict" statements reflect my judgement of which of the oxygen hypotheses conflict directly with which of the phlogiston theories. . . . When ECHO runs this network, starting with all hypotheses at activation .01, it quickly favors the oxygen hypotheses, giving them activations greater than 0. In contrast, all of the phlogiston hypotheses become deactivated. . . .

Lavoisier's argument represents a relatively simple application of ECHO, showing two sets of hypotheses competing to explain the evidence. But more complex explanatory relations can also be important. Sometimes a hypothesis that explains the evidence is itself explained by another hypothesis. Depending on the warrant for the higher-level hypothesis, this extra explanatory layer can increase acceptability: A hypothesis gains from being explained as well as by explaining the evidence. The Lavoisier example does not exhibit this kind of coherence, because neither Lavoisier nor the phlogiston theorists attempted to explain their hypotheses using higher-level hypotheses; nor does the example display the role that analogy can play in explanatory coherence [Thagard, 1989, pp. 445–446].

ECHO Applied to the Scientific Explanatory Reasoning of Darwin

The power of ECHO to evaluate competing scientific arguments is demonstrated in the following comparison of evolutionary and creationist theories.

Both these aspects—coherence based on being explained and on analogy— were important in Darwin's argument for his theory of evolution by natural selection (Darwin 1962). His two most important hypotheses were:

DH2—Organic beings undergo natural selection.
DH3—Species of organic beings have evolved.

These hypotheses together enabled him to explain a host of facts, from the geographical distribution of similar species to existence of vestigial organs. Darwin's argument was explicitly comparative: There are numerous places in the *Origin* where he points to phenomena that his theory explains

TABLE 5.1

Input Propositions For Lavoisier (1862) Example.

Evidence

(proposition 'E1	"In combustion, heat and light are given off.")
(proposition 'E2	"Inflammability is transmittable from one body to another.")
(proposition 'E3	"Combustion only occurs in the presence of pure air.")
(proposition 'E4	"Increase in weight of a burned body is exactly equal to the weight of the air absorbed .")
(proposition 'E5	"Metals undergo calcination.")
(proposition 'E6	"In calcination, bodies increase weight.")
(proposition 'E7	"In calcination, volume of air diminishes.")
(proposition 'E8	"In reduction, effervescence appears.")

Oxygen Hypotheses

(proposition 'OH1	"Pure air contains oxygen principle.")
(proposition 'OH2	"Pure air contains matter of fire and heat.")
(proposition 'OH3	"In combustion, oxygen from the air combines with the burning body.")
(proposition 'OH4	"Oxygen has weight.")
(proposition 'OH5	"In calcination, metals add oxygen to become calxes.")
(proposition 'OH6	"In reduction, oxygen is given off.")

Phlogiston Hypotheses

(proposition 'PH1	"Combustible bodies contain phlogiston.")
(proposition 'PH2	"Combustible bodies contain matter of heat.")
(proposition 'PH3	"In combustion, phlogiston is given off.")
(proposition 'PH4	"Phlogiston can pass from one body to another.")
(proposition 'PH5	"Metals contain phlogiston.")
(proposition 'PH6	"In combustion, phlogiston is given off.")

Source: Thagard, 1989, p. 444.

but that are inexplicable on the generally accepted rival hypothesis that species were separately created by God.

Darwin's two main hypotheses were not simply cohypotheses, however, for he also used DH2 to explain DH3! That is, natural selection explains why species evolve: If populations of animals vary, and natural selection picks out those with features well adapted to particular environments, then new species will arise. Moreover, he offers a Malthusian explanation for why natural selection occurs as the result of the geometrical rate of population growth contrasted with the arithmetical rate of increase in land and food. Thus Malthusian principles explain why evolution occurs, and natural selection and evolution together explain a host of facts better than the competing creation hypothesis does.

TABLE 5.2

Input Explanations and Contradictions in Lavoisier (1862) Example.

Oxygen Explanations
    (explain '(OH1 OH2 OH3) 'E1)
    (explain '(OH1 OH3) 'E3)
    (explain '(OH1 OH3 OH4) 'E4)
    (explain '(OH1 OH5) 'E5)
    (explain '(OH1 OH4 OH5) 'E6)
    (explain '(OH1 OH5) 'E7)
    (explain '(OH1 OH6) 'E8)

Phlogiston Explanations
    (explain '(PH1 PH2 PH3) 'E1)
    (explain '(PH1 PH3 PH4) 'E2)
    (explain '(PH5 PH6) 'E5

Contradictions
    (contradict 'PH3 'OH3)
    (contradict 'PH6 'OH5)

Data
    (data '(E1 E2 E3 E4 E5 E6 E7 E8))

Source: Thagard, 1989, p. 445.

The full picture is even more complicated than this, for Darwin frequently cites the analogy between artificial and natural selection as evidence for his theory. He contends that just as farmers are able to develop new breeds of domesticated animals, so natural selection has produced new species. He uses this analogy not simply to defend natural selection, but also to help in the explanations of the evidence: Particular explanations using natural selection incorporate the analogy with artificial selection. Finally, to complete the picture of explanatory coherence that the Darwin example offers, we must consider the alternative theological explanations that were accepted by even the best scientists until Darwin proposed his theory.

Analysis of *On the Origin of Species* suggests the 15 evidence statements shown in [Table 5.3]. Statements E1–E4 occur in Darwin's discussion of objections to his theory; the others are from the later chapters where he argues for his theory. [Table 5.3] also shows Darwin's main hypotheses. DH2 and DH3 are the core of the theory of evolution by natural selection, providing explanations of its main evidence, E5–E15. DH4–DH6 are auxiliary hypotheses that Darwin uses in resisting objections based on E1–E3.

TABLE 5.3

Explanations and Contradictions for Darwin (1962) Example.

Darwin's Evidence

(proposition 'E1	"The fossil record contains few transitional forms.")
(proposition 'E2	"Animals have complex organs.")
(proposition 'E3	"Animals have instincts.")
(proposition 'E4	"Species when crossed become sterile.")
(proposition 'E5	"Species become extinct.")
(proposition 'E6	"Once extinct, species do not reappear.")
(proposition 'E7	"Forms of life change almost simultaneously around the world.")
(proposition 'E8	"Extinct species are similar to each other and to living forms.")
(proposition 'E9	"Barriers separate similar species.")
(proposition 'E10	"Related species are concentrated in the same areas.")
(proposition 'E11	"Oceanic islands have few inhabitants, often of peculiar species.")
(proposition 'E12	"Species show systematic affinities.")
(proposition 'E13	"Different species share similar morphology.")
(proposition 'E14	"The embryos of different species are similar.")
(proposition 'E15	"Animals have rudimentary and atrophied organs.")

Darwin's Main Hypotheses

(proposition 'DH1	"Organic beings are in a struggle for existence.")
(proposition 'DH2	"Organic beings undergo natural selection.")
(proposition 'DH3	"Species of organic beings have evolved.")

Darwin's Auxiliary Hypotheses

(proposition 'DH4	"The geological record is very imperfect.")
(proposition 'DH5	"There are transitional forms of complex organs.")
(proposition 'DH6	"Mental qualities vary and are inherited.")

Darwin's Facts

(proposition 'DF1	"Domestic animals undergo variation.")
(proposition 'DF2	"Breeders select desired features of animals.")
(proposition 'DF3	"Domestic varieties are developed.")
(proposition 'DF4	"Organic beings in nature undergo variation.")
(proposition 'DF5	"Organic beings increase in population at a high rate.")
(proposition 'DF6	"The sustenance available to organic beings does not increase at a high rate.")
(proposition 'DF7	"Embryos of different domestic varieties are similar.")

Creationist Hypothesis

(proposition 'CH1	"Species were separately created by God.")

Source: Thagard, 1989, p. 448.

He considers the objections concerning the absence of transitional forms to be particularly serious, but explains it away by saying the geological record is so imperfect that we should not expect to find fossil evidence of the many intermediate species his theory requires. . . . The creationist opposition frequently mentioned by Darwin is represented by the single hypothesis that species were separately created by God.

[Table 5.4] shows the explanation and contradiction statements that ECHO uses to set up its network. . . . [There is a] hierarchy of explanations, with the high rate of population increase explaining the struggle for existence, which explains natural selection, which explains evolution. Natural selection and evolution together explain many pieces of evidence. The final component of Darwin's argument is the analogy between natural and artificial selection. . . . Just as breeders' actions explain the development of domestic varieties, so natural selection explains the evolution of species. At another level, Darwin sees an embryological analogy. The embryos of different domestic varieties are quite similar to each other, which is explained by the fact that breeders do not select for properties of embryos. Similarly, nature does not select for most properties of embryos, which explains the similarities between embryos of different species.

Darwin's discussion of objections suggests that he thought creationism could naturally explain the absence of transitional forms and the existence of complex organs and instincts. Darwin's argument was challenged in many ways, but based on his own view of the relevant explanatory relations, at least, the theory of evolution by natural selection is far more coherent that the creation hypothesis. Creationists, of course, would marshal different arguments. . . . Running ECHO to adjust the network to maximize harmony produces the expected result: Darwin's hypotheses are all activated, whereas the creation hypothesis is deactivated. In particular, the hypothesis DH3—that species evolved—reached an asymptote at .921, while the creation hypothesis, CH1, declines to −.491. DH3 accrues activation in three ways. It gains activation from above, from being explained by natural selection, which is derived from the struggle for existence, and from below, by virtue of the many pieces of evidence that it helps to explain. In addition, it receives activation by virtue of the sideways, analogy-based links with explanations using artificial selection. . . .

The Lavoisier and Darwin examples show that ECHO can handle very complex examples of actual scientific reasoning. One might object that in basing ECHO analyses on written texts, I have been modeling the rhetoric of the scientists, not their cognitive processes. Presumably, however, there is some correlation between what we write and what we think. ECHO could be equally well applied to explanatory relations that were asserted in the heat of verbal debate among scientists. Ranney and Thagard (1988) describe ECHO's simulation of naive subjects learning physics, where the inputs to ECHO were based on verbal protocols [Thagard, 1989, pp. 446–449].

TABLE 5.4

Explanations and Contradictions for Darwin Example.

Darwin's Explanations
    (a) of natural selection and evolution
    (explain '(DF5 DF6) 'DH1)
    (explain '(DH1 DF4) 'DH2)
    (explain '(DH2) 'DH3)
    (b) of potential counterevidence
    (explain '(DH2 DH3 DH4) 'E1)
    (explain '(DH2 DH3 DH5) 'E2)
    (explain '(DH2 DH3 DH6) 'E3)
    (c) of diverse evidence
    (explain '(DH2) 'E5)
    (explain '(DH2 DH3) 'E6)
    (explain '(DH2 DH3) 'E7)
    (explain '(DH2 DH3) 'E8)
    (explain '(DH2 DH3) 'E9)
    (explain '(DH2 DH3) 'E10)
    (explain '(DH2 DH3) 'E11)
    (explain '(DH2 DH3) 'E12)
    (explain '(DH2 DH3) 'E13)
    (explain '(DH2 DH3) 'E14)
    (explain '(DH2 DH3) 'E15)
Darwin's Analogies
    (explain '(DF2) 'DF3)
    (explain '(DF2) 'DF7)
    (analogous '(DF2 DH2) '(DF3 DH3))
    (analogous '(DF2 DH2) '(DF7 E14))
Creationist Explanations
    (explain '(CH1) 'E1)
    (explain '(CH1) 'E2)
    (explain '(CH1) 'E3)
    (explain '(CH1) 'E4)
Contradiction
    (contradict 'CH1 'DH3)
Data
    (data '(E1 E2 E3 E4 E5 E6 E7 E8 E9 E10 E11 E12 E13 E14 E15))
    (data '(DF1 DF2 DF3 DF4 DF5 DF6 DF7))

Source: Thagard, 1989, p. 449.

ECHO as a Psychological Model of Belief Change

The psychological validity of ECHO as a model of belief change has been experimentally investigated by Ranney and Thagard (1988). A brief summary of this research is given in the following section.

> Ranney and Thagard (1988) describe the use of ECHO to model the inferences made by naive subjects learning elementary physics by using feedback provided on a computer display (Ranney, 1987). Subjects were asked to predict the motion of several projectiles and then explain these predictions. Analysis of verbal protocol data indicate that subjects sometimes underwent dramatic belief revisions while offering predictions or receiving empirical feedback. ECHO was applied to two particularly interesting cases of belief revision with propositions and explanatory relations based on the verbal protocols. The simulations captured well the dynamics of belief change as new evidence was added to shift the explanatory coherence of the set of propositions [Thagard, 1989, p. 461].

The Theory of Explanatory Coherence: Scope and Power

Thagard provides the following summary account of the major strengths of the theory of explanatory coherence and the ECHO system.

> I conclude with a brief summary of the chief accomplishments of the theory of explanatory coherence offered here.
>
> First, it fits directly with the actual arguments of scientists such as Lavoisier and Darwin who explicitly discuss what competing theories explain. There is no need to postulate probabilities or contrive deductive relations. The theory and ECHO have engendered a far more detailed analysis of these arguments than is typically given by proponents of other accounts. Using the same principles, it applies to important cases of legal reasoning as well.
>
> Second, unlike most accounts of theory evaluation, this view based on explanatory coherence is inherently comparative. If two hypotheses contradict each other, they incohere, so the subsystems of propositions to which they belong will compete with each other. As ECHO shows, successful subsystems of hypotheses and evidence can emerge gracefully from local judgements of explanatory coherence.
>
> Third, the theory of explanatory coherence permits a smooth integration of diverse criteria such as explanatory breadth, simplicity, and analogy. *ECHO's connectionist algorithm shows the computability of coherence relations. The success of the program is best attributed to the usefulness of the connectionist architectures for achieving parallel constraint satisfaction, and to the fact that the problem inherent in inference to the best explanation is the need to satisfy multiple constraints simultaneously.* Not all computational problems are best ap-

proached this way, but parallel constraint satisfaction has proven to be very powerful for other problems as well—for example, analogical mapping (Holyoak and Thagard, 1989).

Finally, my theory surmounts the problem of holism. The principles of explanatory coherence establish pairwise relations of coherence between propositions in an explanatory system. Thanks to ECHO, we know that there is an efficient algorithm for adjusting a system of propositions to turn coherence relations into judgements of acceptability. The algorithm allows every proposition to influence every other one, because there is typically a path of links between any two units, but the influences are set up systematically to reflect explanatory relations. Theory assessment is done as a whole, but a theory does not have to be rejected or accepted as a whole. Those hypotheses that participate in many explanations will be much more coherent with the evidence, and with each other, and will therefore be harder to reject. More peripheral hypotheses may be deactivated even if the rest of the theory they are linked to wins. We thus get a holistic account of inference that can nevertheless differentiate between strong and weak hypotheses. Although our hypotheses face evidence only as a corporate body, evidence and relations of explanatory coherence suffice to separate good hypotheses from bad [Thagard, 1989, p. 465, italics added].

Commentary

There are two primary ways in which to establish the significance of the theory of explanatory coherence and the ECHO system. The first regards the adequacy of ECHO as a model of human explanatory reasoning. The second regards its adequacy as a computational approach to explanatory reasoning.

ECHO as a Model of Human Explanatory Reasoning

Human explanatory reasoning involves both conscious, symbolic, intentional, and serial processing and unconscious, implicit, emergent, and parallel processing. ECHO cannot serve as a model of the former set of characteristics, but as a connectionist architecture it may serve as an approximation to the latter set of characteristics.

ECHO as a Computational Approach To Explanatory Reasoning

ECHO appears to be an important computational approach to establishing the coherence of hypotheses and evidence. ECHO accomplishes its integrated function by means of an algorithm that meets the requirements of parallel constraint satisfaction.

ECHO is a computational mechanism that embodies the basic principles of the theory of explanatory coherence. ECHO and its underlying theory can be evaluated against the criterion of generality of application. Table 5.5 demonstrates generality across the domains of scientific and everyday explanatory reasoning.

TABLE 5.5

The Generality of Intelligent Explanatory Reasoning: Applications of ECHO.

Application of ECHO	Reference
Evaluation of the oxygen theory versus the phlogiston theory (Lavoisier)	Thagard (1989)
Evaluation of evolutionary theory versus creationist theory (Darwin)	Thagard (1989)
Evaluation of theories concerning extinction of the dinosaurs	Thagard (1988b)
Evaluation of theories concerning continental drift	Thagard & Nowak (1988; in press)
Application of problem solving in physics	Ranney & Thagard (1988)
Evaluation of Copernican astronomy versus Ptolemaic astronomy	Nowak & Thagard (forthcoming)
Evaluation of legal reasoning	Thagard (1989)
Evaluation of text comprehension	Shank & Ranney (1991)
Evaluation of belief revision in naive physics	Shank & Ranney (1992)
Evaluation of adversarial argumentation	Thagard (1993)
Perception of social relationships	Miller & Reed (1991); Reed & Marcus-Newell (1991)
Evaluation of debate between Newton and DeCarr	Nowak (in press-b)

6

The Generality of Symbolic Connectionist Models in Intelligent Reasoning

The General Theory and Symbolic-Connectionist Paradigms

A general unified theory of intelligence would need to be inclusive of a dual typology of human cognition and a dual typology of computational models. Deliberative human thought as represented by reasoning, problem solving, planning, judgment, and decision making is distinguished from automatic human memory as represented by retrieval and recognition processes. The first set of cognitive activities is best modeled by symbolic computational models, the second by connectionist computational models. A complete account of cognition will require an integration of the symbolic and connectionist architectures. *In the general unified theory of intelligence, both the cognition and the models have their ultimate foundation in the logic of implication.*

Holyoak and Spellman (1993) provide a useful account of integrated symbolic-connectionist architectures.

> The fact that human cognition has both symbolic and subsymbolic aspects encourages various attempts to integrate the approaches. A number of suggestions for hybrid "symbolic connectionist" models have been offered (e.g., Dyer, 1991; Holyoak, 1991; Minsky, 1991). These models can be divided roughly into two classes. One class of models maintains a core of "traditional" symbolic machinery (e.g., discrete propositions and rules) to represent relation structures, while adding connectionist-style mechanisms for "soft" constraint satisfaction. The second class of models seeks

to develop connectionist representations of relation structures by introducing techniques for handling the binding of objects to rules. We review examples of each of these approaches to integrating the two theoretical perspectives.

Soft Constraint Satisfaction in Reasoning

The generation and evaluation of beliefs—the central task of induction—has a holistic quality that has posed grave difficulty for theoretical treatments. Tweney (1990) identified the complex interrelatedness of hypotheses as a major challenge for computational theories of scientific reasoning. Fodor (1983) has taken the pessimistic position that little progress is to be expected in understanding central cognition because the facts relevant to any belief cannot be circumscribed (i.e, we do not operate within a closed world) and the degree of confirmation of any hypothesis is sensitive to properties of the whole system of beliefs. As Quine (1961:41) put it, "our statements about the external world face the tribunal of sense experience not individually but only as a corporate body." A psychological theory of induction must identify mechanisms that can cope with the holistic quality of hypothesis evaluation (Holland et al., 1986).

One mechanism with the requisite properties is parallel constraint satisfaction, a basic capability of connectionist models. In a connectionist network, local computations involving individual units interact to generate stable global patterns of activity over the entire network. Models that perform "soft" constraint satisfaction over units corresponding to relation structures can attempt to capitalize on the complementary strengths of symbolic representation and connectionist processing. Such symbolic-connectionist models can make inferences based on incomplete information, which standard symbolic systems are often unable to do, using knowledge that distributed connectionist systems cannot readily represent. Models of this sort have been used to account for psychological data concerning text comprehension, analogical reasoning, and evaluation of explanations.

Kintsch (1988) has developed a symbolic-connectionist model to deal with the resolution of ambiguities during text comprehension. His "construction-integration" model has four main components: 1. initial parallel activation of memory concepts corresponding to words in the text, together with formation of propositions by parsing rules; 2. spreading of activation to a small number of close associates of the text concepts; 3. inferring additional propositions by inference rules; and 4. creating excitatory and inhibitory links, with associated weights, between units representing activated concepts and propositions, and allowing the network to settle. The entire process is iterative. A small portion of text is processed, the units active after the settling process are maintained, and then the cycle is repeated with the next portion of text. In addition to accounting for psycholinguistic data in text comprehension, the construction integration model has been extended to simulate levels of expertise in planning routine computing tasks (Mannes and Kintsch, 1991).

Symbolic-connectionist models have been developed to account for two of the basic processes in analogical reasoning—retrieving useful analogs from memory and mapping the elements of a known situation (the source analog) and a new situation (the target analog) to identify useful correspondences. Because analogical mapping requires finding correspondences on the basis of relation structure, most distributed connectionist models lack the requisite representational tools to do it. Purely symbolic models have difficulty avoiding combinatorial explosion when searching for possible analogs in a large memory store and when searching for optimal mappings between two analogs. The symbolic-connectionist models—the ACME model of Holyoak and Thagard (1989), which does analogical mapping, and the ARCS model of Thagard et al. (1990), which does analogical retrieval—operate by taking symbolic, predicate-calculus-style representations of situations as inputs, applying a small set of abstract constraints to build a network of units representing possible mappings between elements of two analogs, and then allowing parallel constraint satisfaction to settle the network into a stable state in which asymptotic activations of units reflect degree of confidence in possible mappings. The constraints on mapping lead to preferences for sets of mapping hypotheses that yield isomorphic correspondences, link similar elements, and map elements of special importance. These same constraints (with differing relative impacts) operate in both the mapping and retrieval models. The mapping model has been applied successfully to model human judgments about complex naturalistic analogies (Spellman and Holyoak, 1992) and has been extended to account for data concerning analogical transfer in mathematical problem solving (Holyoak et al., 1993). . . .

Thagard (1989, 1992) has shown that the problem of evaluating competing explanations can be addressed by a symbolic-connectionist model of explanatory coherence, ECHO. The model takes as input symbolic representations of basic explanatory relations between propositions corresponding to data and explanatory hypotheses. The system then builds a constraint network linking units representing the propositions, using a small number of very general constraints that support explanations with greater explanatory breadth (more links to data), greater simplicity (fewer constituent assumptions), and greater correspondence to analogous explanations of other phenomena. Relations of mutual coherence (modeled by symmetrical excitatory links) hold between hypotheses and the data they explain; relations of competition (inhibitory links) hold between rival hypotheses. Parallel constraint satisfaction settles the network into an asymptotic state in which units representing the most mutually coherent hypotheses and data are active and units representing inconsistent rivals are deactivated. Thagard (1989) showed that ECHO can model a number of realistic cases of explanation evaluation in both scientific and legal contexts; Schank and Ranney (1991, 1992; Ranney, 1993) have used the model to account for students' belief revision in the context of physics problems; and Read and Marcus-Newell (1993) have applied the model to the evaluation of everyday events. . . .

Reflexive Reasoning Using Dynamic Binding

Whereas the models discussed above involve various hybridizations of connectionist processing mechanisms and symbolic representations, a second class of models attempts to provide pure connectionist-style representations of complex relational knowledge. . . . Shastri and Ajjanagadde (1993) have developed a detailed computational model that uses temporal dynamics to code the relation structure of propositions and rules. Dynamic bindings in working memory are represented by units firing in phase. Consider a proposition such as "John gave the book to Mary." On a single phase, the unit representing the object John will fire in synchrony with a unit representing the "giver" role; in a different phase the unit for Mary will fire in synchrony with a unit for the "recipient" role. The system is object-based, in the sense that each time, a slice is occupied by the firing of a single active object unit together with units for all the argument roles that the object fills. Bindings are systematically propagated to make inferences by means of links between units for argument slots. For example, in a rule stating that "If someone receives something, then they own it" the "recipient" role in the antecedent of the rule will be connected to the "owner" role in the consequent. Accordingly, if Mary is dynamically bound to the "recipient" role (by phase locking firing of the "Mary" and "recipient" units), then Mary will become bound to the "owner" role as well (i.e., the unit for Mary will fire in phase with units for *both* relevant roles). Shastri and Ajjanagadde show that their model can answer questions based on inference rules in time that is linear with the length of the inference chain but independent of the number of rules in memory—the most efficient performance pattern theoretically possible.

Shastri and Ajjanagadde (1993) note a number of interesting psychological implications of their dynamic binding model. In particular, they distinguish between two forms of reasoning, which they term "reflexive" and "reflective." Reflexive reasoning is based on spontaneous and efficient inferences drawn in the course of everyday understanding, whereas reflective reasoning is the deliberate and effortful deliberation required in conscious planning and problem solving. It is intriguing that humans are far better at text comprehension than, for example, syllogistic reasoning, even though the formal logical complexity of the former task is much greater than that of the latter (Stenning and Oaksford, 1993). In terms of the Shastri and Ajjanagadde model, text comprehension mainly involves reflexive reasoning, whereas syllogistic inference requires reflective reasoning. Fluent comprehension draws upon a rich network of stored rules, which are used in conjunction with the input to establish a coherent, elaborated model of the situation. Reflexive reasoning of the sort involved in ordinary comprehension relies on dynamic binding of objects to argument slots in preexisting rules. These rules have been encoded into long-term memory, with appropriate interconnections between their arguments. In contrast, reflective reasoning requires manipulation of knowledge in absence of relevant prestored rules. An arbitrary deductive syllogism (e.g., "If all artists are beekeepers, and some beekeepers are chemists, what follows?") is unrelated to any stored rules; rather, understanding the premises requires setting up de novo "rules" (e.g., "If someone is an artist, then that person is a beekeeper") for each problem.

Shastri and Ajjanagadde's model predicts that reflexive reasoning will be constrained by limits on the number of multiply-instantiated predicates, as well as by patterns of variable repetition across the arguments of a rule. The model also makes predictions about the limits of the information that can be active simultaneously in working memory. Although the number of active argument units is potentially unlimited, the number of objects that can be reasoned about in a single session is limited to the number of distinct phases available (because only one object unit may fire in a single phase). Given plausible assumptions about the speed of neural activity, this limit on the number of active objects can be calculated as being five or fewer. This figure is strikingly similar to Miller's (1956) estimate of short-term memory capacity and is consistent with work by Halford and Wilson (1980) indicating that adults cannot simultaneously represent relations involving more than four elements. For example, recent empirical evidence (described by Halford et al., 1993) confirms a limit that will be recognized by anyone who has worked with statistical interactions: The most complex statistical relation that people can deal with in working memory is a 3-way interaction (which involves three independent variables and one dependent variable, for a total of four dimensions). Experimental studies of people's memory for bindings between individuals and properties have revealed similar capacity limits, as well as error patterns consistent with distributed representations of bindings (Stenning and Levy, 1988; Stenning et al., 1988). Recent work has extended the temporal-synchrony approach to other forms of reasoning. Hummel and Holyoak (1992) have shown that the principles embodied in Holyoak and Thagard's (1989) ACME model of analogical mapping can be captured by a model that encodes propositional structure by temporal synchrony.

An interesting feature of the synchrony approach is that the need to minimize "cross talk" between the constituents of relation structures encourages postulating specific types of serial processing at the "micro" level of temporal phases. For example, in the Shastri and Ajjanagadde model, only one object is allowed to fire in each time slice. *It is noteworthy that their model combines localist representations of concepts with distributed control, and thus exemplifies a theoretical "middle ground" between traditional production systems and fully distributed connectionist networks. It is possible that attempts to develop connectionist models of symbol systems will cast new light on the limits of parallel information processing. In addition, connectionist models may provide more effective implementations of the flexible recognition processes based on long-term memory that appear crucial to expertise (Chase and Simon, 1973). More generally, the confluence of the symbolic and connectionist paradigms seems likely to deepen our understanding of the kinds of computations that constitute human thinking* [Holyoak and Spellman, 1993, pp. 272–277, italics added].

7

The Generality of the SOAR System in Intelligent Reasoning

Theories of Unified Cognition

Newell's Unified Theory and the SOAR Research Project

In the following passage from his theoretical and research volume, "Unified Theories of Cognition," Newell (1990) presents his position on the unitary nature of cognition as derivative from a small set of basic mechanisms.

> Psychology has arrived at the possibility of unified theories of cognition—theories that gain their power by having a single system of mechanisms that operate together to produce the full range of cognition.
>   I do not say they are here. But they are within reach and we should strive to attain them (Newell, 1990, p. 1].

The "single system of mechanisms" is a central objective of the SOAR research program (Rosenbloom, Laird, Newell, and McCarl, 1991).

Theoretical Background of SOAR

Rosenbloom, Laird, Newell, and McCarl (1991) discuss the general theoretical background of the SOAR system and its relationship to human and artificial intelligence.

The central scientific problem of artificial intelligence (AI) is to understand what constitutes intelligent action and what processing organizations are capable of such action. Human intelligence—which stands before us like a holy grail— shows to first observation what can only be termed *general intelligence.* A single human exhibits a bewildering diversity of intelligent behavior. The types of goals that humans can set for themselves or accept from the environment seem boundless. Further observation, of course, shows limits to this capacity in any individual—problems range from easy to hard, and problems can always be found that are too hard to be solved. But the general point is still compelling.

Work in AI has already contributed substantially to our knowledge of what functions are required to produce general intelligence. There is substantial, though certainly not unanimous, agreement about some functions that need to be supported: symbols and goal structures, for example. Less agreement exists about what mechanisms are appropriate to support these functions, in large part because such matters depend strongly on the rest of the system and on cost-benefit tradeoffs. Much of this work has been done under the rubric of AI tools and languages, rather than AI systems themselves. However, it takes only a slight shift of viewpoint to change from what is an aid for the programmer to what is structure for the intelligent system itself. Not all features survive this transformation, but enough do to make the development of AI languages as much substantial research as tool building. These proposals provide substantial ground on which to build.

The SOAR project has been building on this foundation in an attempt to understand the functionality required to support general intelligence. Our current understanding is embodied in the SOAR architecture (Laird, 1986; Laird, Newell, and Rosenbloom, 1986) [Rosenbloom, Laird, Newell, and McCarl, 1991, pp. 289–290, italics added].

General Intelligence and Levels of Description

Rosenbloom, Laird, Newell, and McCarl (1991) analyze general intelligence at several levels of description, employing the concepts of cognitive, neural, and logical bands.

The idea of analyzing systems in terms of multiple levels of description is a familiar one in computer science. In one version, computer systems are described as a sequence of levels that starts at the bottom with the device works up through the circuit level, the logic level, and then one or more program levels. Each level provides a description of the system at some level of abstraction. The sequence is built up by defining each higher level in terms of the structure provided at the lower levels. This idea has also recently been used to analyze human cognition in terms of levels of description (Newell, 1990). Each level corresponds to a particular time scale, such as ~ 100 msec. and ~ 1 sec., with a new level occurring for each new order of magnitude. *The four levels between ~10 msec. and ~10 sec.*

comprise the cognitive band [Fig 7.1]. The lowest cognitive level—at ~10 msec.—is the symbol-accessing level, where the knowledge referred to by symbols is retrievable. The second cognitive level—at ~100 msec.—is the level at which elementary deliberate operations occur; that is, the level at which encoded knowledge is brought to bear, and the most elementary choices are made. The third and fourth cognitive levels—at ~1 sec. and ~10 sec.—are the simple-operator-composition and goal-attainment levels. At these levels, sequences of deliberations can be composed to achieve goals. *Above the cognitive band is the rational band, at which the system can be described as being goal oriented, knowledge-based, and strongly adaptive. Below the cognitive band is the neural band.*

[We] describe SOAR as a sequence of three cognitive levels: the memory level, at which symbol accessing occurs; the decision level, at which elementary deliberate operations occur; and the goal level, at which goals are set and achieved via sequences of decisions. The goal level is an amalgamation of the top two cognitive levels from the analysis of human cognition.

In this description we will often have call to describe mechanisms that are built into the architecture of the SOAR. *The architecture consists of all of the fixed structure of the SOAR system. According to the levels analysis, the correct view to be taken of this fixed structure is that it comprises the set of mechanisms provided by the levels underneath the cognitive band. For human*

FIGURE 7.1

Partial Hierarchy of Time Scales in Human Cognition.

The SOAR architecture as a basis for general intelligence

Rational Band   . . .

	~ 10 sec.	Goal attainment
Cognitive Band	~ 1 sec.	Simple operator composition
	~ 100 msec.	Elementary deliberate operations
	~ 10 msec.	Symbol accessing

Neural Band   . . .

Source: Rosenbloom, P.S., Laird, J.E., Newell, A., & McCarl, R. (1991). A Preliminary Analysis of the SOAR Architecture as a Basis for General Intelligence. Artificial Intelligence, 47, 289-325.
Reprinted with the permission of the Elsevier Science Publishers.

*cognition this is the neural band. For artificial cognition, this may be a con-
nectionist band, though it need not be. This view notwithstanding, it should be
remembered that it is the SOAR architecture which is primary in our research.
The use of the levels viewpoint is simply an attempt at imposing a particular,
hopefully illuminating, theoretical structure on top of the existing architecture*
[Rosenbloom, Laird, Newell, and McCarl, 1991, pp. 290–291, italics added].

SOAR: The First Methodological Assumption

The development of SOAR rests on four methodological assumptions
(see [Table 7.1]). The first of these four assumptions is described in the
following section.

*The first assumption is the utility of focusing on the cognitive band, as opposed
to the neural or rational bands. This is a view that has traditionally been shared
by a large segment of the cognitive science community; it is not, however, shared
by the connectionist community, which focuses on the neural band (plus the lower
levels of the cognitive band), or by the logicist and expert-systems communities,
which focus on the rational band. This assumption is not meant to be exclusionary,
as a complete understanding of general intelligence requires the understanding
of all these descriptive bands* (Investigations of the relationship of SOAR to

TABLE 7.1

SOAR's Methodological Assumptions

---

1. General intelligence comprises neural, cognitive, and rational levels or
bands. SOAR concentrates on the cognitive band.

2. A theory of general intelligence embraces both human and artificial
intelligence.

3. The intelligence of SOAR results from a small set of mechanisms.

4. Research should utilize SOAR's existing mechanisms in exploring new
areas of application rather than adding new mechanisms.

Source: Rosenbloom, P.S., Laird, J.E., Newell, A., & McCarl, R.
(1991). A Preliminary Analysis of the SOAR Architecture as a
Basis for General Intelligence. Artificial Intelligence, 47, 289-
325. Reprinted with the permission of the Elsevier Science
Publishers.

the neural and rational bands can be found in Newell, 1990; Rosenbloom, 1989; and Rosenbloom, Laird, and Newell, 1990). Instead the assumption is that there is important work to be done by focusing on the cognitive band. One reason is that, as just mentioned, a complete model of general intelligence will require a model of the cognitive band. A second reason is that an understanding of the cognitive band can constrain models of the neural and rational bands. A third, more applied reason, is that a model of the cognitive band is required in order to be able to build practical intelligence systems. Neural-band models need the higher levels of organization that are provided by the cognitive band in order to reach complex task performance. Rational-band models need the heuristic adequacy provided by the cognitive band in order to be computationally feasible. *A fourth reason is that there is a wealth of both psychological and AI data about the cognitive band that can be used as the basis for elucidating the structure of its levels. This data can help us understand what type of symbolic architecture is required to support general intelligence* [Rosenbloom, Laird, Newell, and McCarl, 1991, pp. 291–292, italics added].

SOAR: The Second Methodological Assumption

The second methodological assumption concerns the benefits that accrue from a conception of general intelligence that includes both human and artificial intelligence.

The second assumption is that general intelligence can most usefully be studied by not making a distinction between human and artificial intelligence. The advantage of this assumption is that it allows wider ranges of research methodologies and data to be brought to bear to mutually constrain the structure of the system. Our research methodology includes a mixture of experimental data, theoretical justifications, and comparative studies in both artificial intelligence and cognitive psychology. Human experiments provide data about performance universals and limitations that may reflect the structure of the architecture. For example, the ubiquitous power law of practice—the time to perform a task is a power-law function of the number of times the task has been performed—was used to generate a model of human practice (Newell and Rosenbloom, 1981; Rosenbloom and Newell, 1986), which later converted into a proposal for a general artificial learning mechanism (Laird, Rosenbloom, and Newell, 1984, 1986; Steier et al., 1988). Artificial experimentals—the application of implemented systems to a variety of tasks requiring intelligence—provide sufficient feedback about the mechanisms embodied in the architecture and their interactions (Hsu, Prietula and Steier, 1988; Rosenbloom et al., 1985; Steier, 1987; Steier and Newell, 1988; Washington and Rosenbloom, 1988). Theoretical justifications attempt to provide an abstract analysis of the requirements of intelligence, and of how various architectural mechanisms fulfill those requirements (Newell, 1990; Newell, Rosenbloom, and Laird, 1989; Rosenbloom, 1989; Rosenbloom, Laird, and Newell, 1988; Rosenbloom, Newell, and Laird,

1990). Comparative studies, pitting one system against another, provide an evaluation of how well the respective systems perform, as well as insight about how the capabilities of one of the systems can be incorporated in the other (Etzioni and Mitchell, 1989; Rosenbloom and Laird, 1986) [Rosenbloom, Laird, Newell, and McCarl, 1991, p. 292, italics added].

SOAR: The Third Methodological Assumption

The third methodological assumption posits a small set of mechanisms to be sufficient for the SOAR architecture to function intelligently.

The third assumption is that the architecture should consist of a small set of orthogonal mechanisms. All intelligent behaviors should involve all, or nearly all, of these basic mechanisms. This assumption biases the development of SOAR strongly in the direction of uniformity and simplicity, and away from modularity (Fodor, 1983) and toolkit approaches. When attempting to achieve a new functionality in SOAR, the first step is to determine in what ways the existing mechanisms can already provide the functionality. This can force the development of new solutions to old problems, and reveal new connections—through the common underlying mechanisms—among previously distinct capabilities (Rosenbloom, Laird, and Newell, 1988). Only if there is no appropriate way to achieve the new functionality are new mechanisms considered [Rosenbloom, Laird, Newell, and McCarl, 1991, p. 293, italics added].

SOAR: The Fourth Methodological Assumption

The fourth methodological assumption is that the SOAR system should be maximally stretched to expand its range of intelligent performance.

The fourth assumption is that architectures should be pushed to the extreme to evaluate how much of general intelligence they can cover. A serious attempt at evaluating the coverage of an architecture involves a long-term commitment by an extensive research group. Much of the research involves the apparently mundane activity of replicating classical results within the architecture. Sometimes these demonstrations will by necessity be strict replications, but often the architecture will reveal novel approaches, provide a deeper understanding of the result and test relationship to other results, or provide the means of going beyond what was done in the classical work. *As these results accumulate over time, along with other more novel results, the system gradually approaches the ultimate goal of general intelligence* [Rosenbloom, Laird, Newell, and McCarl, 1991, p. 293, italics added].

Structure of SOAR: Memory Level

SOAR's declarative, procedural, control, and episodic knowledge are stored in a long-term memory production and can be retrieved for processing in working memory.

Long-Term Memory

Major characteristics of SOAR's long-term memory are described in the following account.

> *A general intelligence requires a memory with a large capacity for the storage of knowledge. A variety of types of knowledge must be stored, including declarative knowledge (facts about the world, including facts about actions that can be performed), procedural knowledge (facts about how to perform actions, and control knowledge about which actions to perform when), and episodic knowledge (which actions were done when).* Any particular task will require some subset of the knowledge stored in the memory. Memory access is the process by which this subset is retrieved for use in task performance.
>
> The lowest level of the SOAR architecture is the level at which these memory phenomena occur. *All of SOAR's long term knowledge is stored in a single production memory. Whether a piece of knowledge represents procedural, declarative, or episodic knowledge, it is stored in one or more productions.* Each production is a condition-action structure that performs its actions when its conditions are met. Memory access consists of the execution of these productions. During the execution of a production, variables in its actions are instantiated with values. Action variables that existed in the conditions are instantiated with the values bound in the conditions. Action variables that did not exist in the conditions act as generators of new symbols [Rosenbloom, Laird, Newell, and McCarl, 1991, pp. 293–294, italics added].

Working Memory

Important features and functions of SOAR's working memory are summarized in the following section.

> *The result of memory access is the retrieval of information into a global working memory. The working memory is a temporary memory that contains all of SOAR's short-term processing context.* Working memory consists of an interrelated set of objects with attribute-value pairs. For example, an object representing a green cat named Fred might look like (objecto025 ^ name fred ^ type cat ^ color green). The symbol o025 is the identifier of the object, a short-term symbol for the object that exists only as long as the object is in working memory. Objects are related by using the identifiers of some objects as attributes and values of other objects.

There is one special type of working memory structure, the preference. Preferences encode control knowledge about the acceptability and desirability of actions, according to a fixed semantics of preference types. Acceptability preferences determine which actions should be considered as candidates. Desirability preferences define a partial ordering on the candidate actions. For example, a better (or alternatively, worse) preference can be used to represent the knowledge that one action is more (or less) desirable than another action, and a best (or worst) preference can be used to represent the knowledge that an action is at least as good (or bad) as every other action [Rosenbloom, Laird, Newell, and McCarl, 1991, p. 294 , italics added].

Memory and Productions

The retrieval operations of SOAR's productions are set forth in the following account.

In a traditional production-system architecture, each production is a problem-solving operator (see, for example, [Nilsson, 1980]). The right-hand side of the production represents some action to be performed, and the left-hand side represents the preconditions for correct application of the action (plus possibly some desirability conditions). One consequence of this view of productions is that the productions must also be the locus of behavioral control. If productions are going to act, it must be possible to control which one executes at each moment; a process known as conflict resolution. In a logic architecture, each production is a logical implication. The meaning of such a production is that if the left-hand side (the antecedent) is true, then so is the right-hand side (the consequent). (The directionality of the implication is reversed in logic programming languages such as Prolog, but the point still holds.) SOAR's productions are neither operators nor implications. Instead, SOAR's productions perform (parallel) memory retrieval. Each production is a retrieval structure for an item in long-term memory. The right-hand side of the rule represents a long-term datum, and the left-hand side represents the situations in which it is appropriate to retrieve that datum into working memory. The traditional production-system and logic notions of action, control, and truth are not directly applicable to SOAR's productions. All control in SOAR is performed at the decision level. *Thus, there is no conflict resolution process in the SOAR production system, and all productions execute in parallel. This all flows directly from the production system being a long-term memory. SOAR separates the retrieval of long-term information from the control of which act to perform next* [Rosenbloom, Laird, Newell, and McCarl, 1991, pp. 294–295, italics added].

Encoding Knowledge in Productions

The rationale for SOAR's method of encoding declarative and procedural knowledge in productions is given in the following passage.

Of course it is possible to encode knowledge of operators and logical implications in the production memory. For example, the knowledge about how to implement a typical operator can be stored procedurally as a set of productions which retrieve the state resulting from the operator's application. The productions' conditions determine when the state is to be retrieved—for example, when the operator is being applied and its preconditions are met. An alternative way to store operator implementation knowledge is declaratively as a set of structures that are completely contained in the actions of one or more productions. The structures describe not only the results of the operator, but also its preconditions. The productions' conditions determine when to retrieve this declarative operator description into working memory. A retrieved operator description must be interpreted by other productions to actually have an affect.

In general, there are these two distinct ways to encode knowledge in the production memory: procedurally and declaratively. If the knowledge is procedurally encoded, then the execution of the production reflects the knowledge, but does not actually retrieve it into working memory—it only retrieves the structures encoded in the actions. On the other hand, if a piece of knowledge is encoded declaratively in the actions of a production, then it is retrievable in its entirety. *This distinction between procedural and declarative encodings of knowledge is distinct from whether the knowledge is declarative (represents facts about the world) or procedural (represents facts about procedures). Moreover, each production can be viewed in either way, either as a procedure which implicitly represents conditional information, or as the indexed storage of declarative structures* [Rosenbloom, Laird, Newell, and McCarl, 1991, p. 295, italics added].

Structure of SOAR: Decision Level

The capacity to execute an appropriate course of action depends on its decision structures and functions as described in the following account.

In addition to a memory, a general intelligence requires the ability to generate and/or select a course of action that is responsive to the current situation. The second level of the SOAR architecture, the decision level, is the level at which this processing is performed. The decision level is based on the memory level plus an architecturally provided, fixed, decision procedure. The decision level proceeds in a two-phase elaborate-decide cycle. During elaboration, the memory is accessed repeatedly, in parallel, until quiescence is reached; that is, until no more productions can execute. This results in the retrieval into working memory of all of the accessible knowledge that is relevant to the current decision. This may include a variety of types of information, but most direct relevance here is knowledge about actions that can be performed and preference knowledge about what actions are acceptable and desirable. After quiescence has occurred, the decision procedure selects one of the retrieved actions based on the preferences that were retrieved into working memory and their fixed semantics.

The decision level is open both with respect to the consideration of arbitrary actions, and with respect to the utilization of arbitrary knowledge in making a selection. This openness allows SOAR to behave in both plan-following and reactive fashions. SOAR is following a plan when a decision is primarily based on previously generated knowledge about what to do. SOAR is being reactive when a decision is based primarily on knowledge about the current situation (as reflected in the working memory) [Rosenbloom, Laird, Newell, and McCarl, 1991, pp. 295–296, italics added].

Structure of SOAR: Goal Level

The nature of goal setting and goal processing is described in the following section.

In addition to being able to make decisions, a general intelligence must also be able to direct this behavior towards some end; that is, it must be able to set and work towards goals. The third level of the SOAR architecture, the goal level, is the level at which goals are processed. This level is based on the decision level. Goals are set whenever a decision cannot be made; that is, when the decision procedure reaches an impasse. Impasses occur when there are no alternatives that can be selected (*no-chance* and *rejection* impasses) or when there are multiple alternatives that can be selected, but insufficient discriminating preferences exist to allow a choice to be made among them (*tie* and *conflict* impasses). Whenever an impasse occurs, the architecture generates the goal of resolving the impasse. Along with this goal, a new *performance context* is created. The creation of a new context allows decisions to continue to be made in the service of achieving the goal of resolving the impasse—nothing can be done in the original context because it is at an impasse. If an impasse now occurs in this subgoal, another new subgoal and performance context are created. This leads to a goal (and context) stack in which the top-level goal is to perform some task, and lower-level goals are to resolve impasses in problem solving. A subgoal is terminated when either its impasse is resolved, or some higher impasse in the stack is resolved (making the subgoal superfluous) [Rosenbloom, Laird, Newell, and McCarl, 1991, p. 296, italics added].

Goals and Problem Spaces

Goal activities are processed in problem spaces, as described in the following account.

In SOAR, all symbolic goal-oriented tasks are formulated in problem spaces. A problem space consists of a set of states and a set of operators. The states represent situations, and the operators represent actions which when applied to states yield other states. Each performance context consists of a goal, plus roles for a problem state, a state, and an operator. Problem solving is driven by decisions that result in the selection of problem spaces, states, and operators for their respective context roles. Given a goal, a problem space should be selected in which goal achievement can be pursued. Then an initial state should be selected that represents the initial situation. Then an operator should be selected for application to the initial state. Then another state should be selected (most likely the result of applying the operator to the previous state). This process continues until a sequence of operators has been discovered that transforms the initial state into a state in which the goal has been achieved. One subtle consequence of the use of problem spaces is that each one implicitly defines a set of constraints on how the task is to be performed. For example, if the Eight Puzzle is attempted in a problem space containing only a slide-tile operator, all solution paths maintain the constraint that the tiles are never picked up off the board. Thus, such conditions need not be tested explicitly in desired states.

Each problem solving decision—the selection of a problem space, a state, or an operator—is based on the knowledge accessible in the production memory. If the knowledge is both correct and sufficient, SOAR exhibits highly controlled behavior; at each decision point the right alternative is selected. Such behavior is accurately described as being algorithmic or knowledge-intensive. However, for a general intelligence faced with a broad array of unpredictable tasks, situations will arise—inevitaby. and indeed frequently—in which the accessible knowledge is either incorrect or insufficient. It is possible that correct decisions will fortuitously be made, but it is more likely that either incorrect decisions will be made or an impasse will occur. If an incorrect decision is made, the system must eventually recover and get itself back on a path to a goal, for example, by backtracking. If instead an impasse occurs, the system must execute a sequence of problem space operators in the resulting subgoal to find (or generate) the information that will allow a decision to be made. This processing may itself be highly algorithmic, if enough control knowledge is available to uniquely determine what to do, or it may involve a large amount of further search.

As described earlier, operator implementation knowledge can be repre- sented procedurally in the production memory, enabling operator im- plementation to be performed directly by memory retrieval. When the operator is selected, a set of productions execute that collectively build up the representation of the result state by combining data from long-term memory and the previous state. This type of implementation is comparable to the conventional implementation of an operator as a fixed piece of code. However, if operator implementation knowledge is stored declaratively, or if no operator implementation knowledge is stored, then a subgoal occurs, and the operator must be implemented by the execution of a sequence of problem space operators in the subgoal. If a declarative description of the to-be-implemented operator is available, then these lower operations may implement the operator by interpreting its declara- tive description (as was demonstrated in work on task acquisition in SOAR (Steier et al., 1987). Otherwise the operator can be implemented by decomposing it into a set of simpler operators for which operator implementation knowledge is available, or which can in turn be decomposed further.

When an operator is implemented in a subgoal, the combination of the operator and the subgoal correspond to the type of deliberately created subgoal common in AI problem solvers. The operator specifies a task to be performed, while the subgoal indicates that accomplishing the task should be treated as a goal for further problem solving. In complex problems, like computer configuration, it is common for there to be complex high-level operators, such as *Configure computer* which are implemented by selecting problem spaces in which they can be decomposed into simpler tasks. Many of the traditional goal management issues—such as conjunction, conflict, and selection—show up as operator management issues in SOAR. For example, a set of conjunctive subgoals can be ordered by ordering operators that later lead to impasses (and subgoals).

As described in [Rosenbloom, Laird, and Newell, 1988], a subgoal not only represents a subtask to be performed, but it also represents an introspective act that allows unlimited amounts of meta-level problem-space processing to be performed. The entire working memory—the goal stack and all information linked to it—is available for examination and augmentation in a subgoal. At any time a production can examine and augment any part of the goal stack. Likewise, a decision can be made at any time for any of the goals in the hierarchy. This allows subgoal problem solving to analyze the situation that led to the impasse, and even to change the subgoal, should it be appropriate. One not uncommon occurrence is for information to be generated within a subgoal that instead of satisfying the subgoal, causes the subgoal to become irrelevant and consequently to disappear. Processing tends to focus on the bottom-most goal because all of the others have reached impasses. However, the processing is completely opportunistic, so that when appropriate information becomes available at a higher level, processing at that level continues immediately and all lower subgoals are terminated [Rosenbloom, Laird, Newell, and McCarl, 1991, pp. 297–298, italics added].

Learning in SOAR

The concept of chunks, their nature, content, and role in learning are summarized in the following account.

All learning occurs by the acquisition of chunks—productions that summarize the problem solving that occurs in subgoals [Laird, Rosenbloom, and Newell, 1986]. The actions of a chunk represent the knowledge generated during the subgoal; that is, the results of the subgoal. The conditions of the chunk represent an access path to this knowledge, consisting of those elements of the parent goals upon which the results depended. The results of the subgoal are determined by finding the elements generated in the subgoal that are available for use in subgoals—an element is a result of a subgoal precisely because it is available to processes outside of the subgoal. The access path is computed by analyzing the traces of the productions that fired in the subgoal—each production trace effectively states that its actions depended on its conditions. This dependency analysis yields a set of conditions that have been implicitly generalized to ignore irrelevant aspects of the situation. The resulting generality allows chunks to transfer to situations other than the one in which it was learned. The primary system-wide effect of chunking is to move SOAR along the space-time trade-off by allowing relevantly similar future decisions to be based on direct retrieval of information from memory rather than on problem solving within a subgoal. If the chunk is used, an impasse will not occur, because the required information is already available.

Care must be taken to not confuse the power of chunking as a learning mechanism with the power of SOAR as a learning system. Chunking is a simple goal-based, dependency-tracing, caching scheme, analogous to explanation-based learning (DeJong and Mooney, 1986; Mitchell, Keller, and Kedar-Cabelli, 1986; Rosenbloom and Laird, 1986) and a variety of other schemes (Rosenbloom and Newell, 1986). *What allows SOAR to exhibit a wide variety of learning behaviors are the variations in the types of subgoals that are chunked; the types of problem solving, in conjunction with the types and sources of knowledge, used in the subgoals; and the ways the chunks are used in later problem solving. The role that a chunk will play is determined by the type of subgoal for which it was learned.* State-no-change, operator-tie, and operator-no-change subgoals lead respectively to state augmentation, operator selection, and operator implementation productions. *The content of a chunk is determined by the types of problem solving and knowledge used in the subgoal. A chunk can lead to knowledge acquisition (or knowledge level learning (Dietterich, 1986)) if it is used to make old/new judgements; that is, to distinguish what has been learned from what has not been learned (Rosenbloom, Laird, and Newell, 1987, 1988, 1990)* [Rosenbloom, Laird, Newell, and McCarl, 1991, pp. 298–299, italics added].

Perception and Motor Control in SOAR

The perceptual motor interface and its relationship to working memory are described in the following section.

One of the most recent functional additions to the SOAR architecture is a perceptual-motor interface (Weismeyer, 1988, 1989). All perceptual and motor behavior is mediated through working memory; specifically, through the state in the top problem solving context. Each distinct perceptual field has a designated attribute of this state to which it adds its information. Likewise, each distinct motor field has a designated attribute of the state from which it takes its commands. The perceptual and motor systems are autonomous with respect to each other and the cognitive system.

Encoding and decoding productions can be used to convert between the high-level structures used by the cognitive system, and the low-level structures used by the perceptual and motor systems. The productions are like ordinary productions, except that they examine only the perceptual and motor fields, and not any of the rest of the context stack. This autonomy from the context stack is critical, because it allows the decision procedure to proceed without waiting for quiescence among the encoding and decoding productions, which may never happen in a rapidly changing environment [Rosenbloom, Laird, Newell, and McCarl, 1991, pp. 299–300].

Default Knowledge in SOAR

The default knowledge in SOAR permits it to resolve impasses in its operations.

SOAR has a set of productions (55 in all) that provide default responses to each of the possible impasses that can arise, and thus prevent the system from dropping into a bottomless pit in which it generates an unbounded number of content-free performance contexts. . . . This allows another candidate operator to be selected, if there is one, or for a different impasse to arise if there are no additional candidates. This default response, as with all of them, can be overridden by additional knowledge if it is available.

One large part of the default knowledge (10 productions) is responsible for setting up large operator subgoaling as the default response to no-change impasses on operators. That is, it attempts to find some other state in the problem space to which the selected operators can be applied. This is accomplished by generating acceptable and worst preferences in the subgoal for the parent problem space. If another problem space is suggested, possibly for implementing the operator, it will be selected. Otherwise, the selection of the parent problem space in the subgoal enables operator subgoaling. A sequence of operators is then applied in the subgoal until a state is generated that satisfies the preconditions of an operator higher in the goal stack.

Another large part of the default knowledge (33 productions) is responsible for setting up lookahead search as the default response to tied impasses. This is accomplished by generating acceptable and worst preferences for the *selection* problem space. The selection problem space consists of operators that evaluate the tied alternatives. Based on the evaluations produced by these operators, default productions create preferences that break the tie and resolve the impasse. In order to apply the evaluation operators, domain knowledge must exist that can create an evaluation. If no such knowledge is available, a second impasse arises—a no-change on the evaluation operator. As mentioned earlier, the default response to an operator no-change impasse is to perform operator subgoaling. However, for a no-change impasse on an evaluation operator this is overridden and a lookahead search is performed instead. The results of the lookahead search are used to evaluate the tied alternatives.

As SOAR is developed, it is expected that more and more knowledge will be included as part of the basic system about how to deal with a variety of situations. For example, one area on which we are currently working is the provision of SOAR with a basic arithmetical capability, including problem spaces for addition, mul-

tiplication, subtraction, division, and comparison. One way of looking at existing default knowledge is as the tip of this large iceberg of backaround knowledge. However, another way to look at the default knowledge is as part of the architecture itself. Some of the default knowledge—how much is still unclear—must be innate rather than learned. The rest of the system's knowledge, such as the arithmetic spaces, should then be learnable from there [Rosenbloom, Laird, Newell, and McCarl, 1991, pp. 300–301, italics added].

SOAR: Task Achievements

SOAR's achievements in search-based tasks are summarized in the following section (see [Table 7.2]).

TABLE 7.2

Examples of SOAR's Task Achievements

Tasks	Examples
Search Based	Broad variety of search methods; hill climbing and depth first search (singly and combined); operator subgoaling and depth first search (singly and combined); range of search methods appropriate for range of problem spaces.
Knowledge based	R1-SOAR computer configuration system; the Cypress-SOAR design system; the Neomycin SOAR medical diagnosis system.
Learning	Learning from success; learning from failure; transfer of learned knowledge in trials and across problems; learning from a variety of sources.

Source: Rosenbloom, P.S., Laird, J.E., Newell, A., & McCarl, R. (1991). A Preliminary Analysis of the SOAR Architecture as a Basis for General Intelligence. Artificial Intelligence, 47, 289-325. Reprinted with the permission of the Elsevier Science Publishers.

Various versions of SOAR have been demonstrated to be able to perform over 30 different search methods (Laird, 1986; Laird and Newell, 1983; Laird, Newell, and Rosenbloom, 1987). SOAR can also exhibit hybrid methods—such as a combination of hill-climbing and depth-first search or of operator subgoaling and depth-first search—and use different search methods for different problem spaces within the same problem [Rosenbloom, Laird, Newell, and McCarl, 1991, p. 310].

SOAR's achievements with knowledge-based tasks are indicated in the following section.

Several knowledge-based tasks have been implemented in SOAR, including RI-SOAR computer configuration system (Rosenbloom et al., 1987), the Cypress-SOAR and Designer-SOAR algorithm design systems (Steier, 1987; Steier and Newell, 1988), the Neomycin-SOAR medical diagnosis system (Washington and Rosenbloom, 1988), and the Merl-SOAR job-shop scheduling system (Hsu, Prietula, and Steier, 1988) [Rosenbloom, Laird, Newell, and McCarl, 1991, pp. 310–311].

SOAR's achievements with learning tasks are discussed in the following section.

The architecture directly supports a form of experiential learning in which chunking compiles goal-level problem solving into memory-level productions. Execution of the productions should have the same effect as the problem solving would have had, just more quickly. The varieties of subgoals for which chunks are learned lead to varieties in types of productions learned: problem space creation and selection; state creation and selection; and operator creation, selections, and execution. An alternative classification for this same set of behaviors is that is covers procedural, episodic and declarative knowledge [Rosenbloom, Newell, and Laird, 1990]. The variations in goal outcomes lead to both learning from success and learning from failure. The ability to learn about all subgoal results leads to learning about important intermediate results, in addition to learning about goal success and failure. The implicit generalization of chunks leads to transfer of learned knowledge to other subtasks within the same problem (within-trial transfer), other instances of the same problem (across-trial transfer), and other problems (across-task transfer). Variations in the types of problems performed in SOAR lead to chunking in knowledge-based tasks, search-based, and robotic tasks. Variations in sources of knowledge lead to learning from both internal and external knowledge sources. A summary of many of the types of learning that have so far been demonstrated in SOAR can be found in [Steier, et al., 1987] [Rosenbloom, Laird, Newell, and McCarl, 1991, p. 311].

SOAR: Source of Its Power

The reasons for SOAR's effectiveness and efficiency are discussed in the following section (see [Table 7.3]).

SOAR's power and flexibility arise from at least four identifiable sources. The first source of power is the universality of the architecture. While it may seem that this should go without saying, it is in fact a crucial factor, and thus important to mention explicitly. Universality provides the primitive capability to perform any computable task, but does not by itself explain why SOAR is more appropriate than any other universal architecture for knowledge-based, search-based, learning, and robotic tasks.

TABLE 7.3

Sources of SOAR's Power and Flexibility

I.   Universality of its architecture

II.   Uniformity of its architecture
      A.   Single type of memory structure
      B.   Single type of task representation: problem spaces
      C.   Single type of decision procedure

III. Specific mechanisms built into its architecture
      A.   Production memory
      B.   Working memory
      C.   Decision procedures and controls
      D.   Subgoals
      E.   Problem spaces
      F.   Chunking
      G.   Perceptual motor system

IV.   The coordination of methods and mechanisms within a unified system
      A.   The combining of weak methods and learning mechanisms
      B.   The combining of strong methods (knowledge) and weak methods (search)

Source: Rosenbloom, P.S., Laird, J.E., Newell, A., & McCarl, R. (1991). A Preliminary Analysis of the SOAR Architecture as a Basis for General Intelligence. Artificial Intelligence, 47, 289-325. Reprinted with the permission of the Elsevier Science Publishers.

The second source of power is the uniformity of the architecture. Having only one type of long-term memory structure allows a single, relatively simple, learning mechanism to behave as a general learning mechanism. Having only one type of task representation (problem spaces) allows SOAR to move continuously from one extreme of brute-force search to the other extreme of knowledge-intensive (or procedural) behavior without having to make any representational decisions. Having only one type of decision procedure allows a single, relatively simple, subgoal mechanism to generate all of the types of subgoals needed by the system. The traditional downside of uniformity is weakness and inefficiency. If instead the system were built up as a set of specialized modules or agents, as proposed in [Fodor, 1983; Minsky, 1986], then each of the modules could be optimized for its own narrow task. Our approach to this issue in SOAR has been to go strongly with uniformity—for all of the benefits listed above—but to achieve efficiency (power) through the addition of knowledge. This knowledge can either be added by hand (programming) or by chunking.

The third source of power is the specific mechanisms incorporated into the architecture. The production memory provides pattern-directed access to large amounts of knowledge; provides the ability to use strong problem solving methods; and provides a memory structure with a small-grained modularity. The working memory allows global access to processing state. The decision procedure provides an open control loop that can react immediately to new situations and knowledge; contributes to the modularity of the memory by allowing access to proceed in an uncontrolled fashion (conflict resolution was a major source of nonmodularity in earlier production systems); provides a flexible control language (preferences); and provides a notion of impasse that is used as the basis for the generation of subgoals. Subgoals focus the system's resources on situations where the accessible knowledge is inadequate, and allow flexible meta-level processing. Problem spaces separate control from action, allowing them (control and action) to be reasoned about independently; provide a constrained context within which the search for a desired state can occur; provide the ability to use weak problem solving methods; and provide for straightforward responses to uncertainty and error (search and backtracking). Chunking acquires long-term knowledge from experience; compiles interpreted procedures into non-interpreted ones; and provides generalization and transfer. The perceptual-motor system provides the ability to observe and affect the external world in parallel with the cognitive activity.

The fourth source of power is the interaction effects that result from the integration of all of the capabilities within a single system. The most compelling results generated so far come about from these interactions. One example comes from the mixture of weak methods, strong methods, and learning that is found in systems like RI-SOAR. Strong methods are based on having knowledge about what to do at each step. Because strong methods tend to be efficient and to produce high-quality solutions, they should be used whenever possible. Weak methods are based on searching to make up for lack of knowledge about what should be done. Such methods contribute robustness and scope by providing the system with a fall-back approach for situations in which the available strong methods do not work. Learning results in the addition of knowledge, turning weak methods into strong ones. For example, in RI-SOAR it was demonstrated how computer configuration could be cast as a search problem, how strong methods (knowledge) could be used to reduce search, how weak methods (subgoals and search) could be used to make up for a lack of knowledge, and how learning could add knowledge as the result of search.

Another interesting interaction effect comes from work on abstraction planning, in which a difficult problem is solved by first learning a plan for an abstract version of the problem, and then using the abstract plan to aid in finding a plan to the full problem [Newell and Simon, 1972; Sacerdoti, 1974; Unruh, Rosenbloom, and Laird, 1987; Unruh and Rosenbloom, 1989]. Chunking helps the abstraction planning process by recording the abstract plan as a set of operator-selection production, and by acquiring other productions that reduce the amount of search required in generating a plan. Abstraction helps the learning process by allowing chunks to be learned more quickly—abstract searches tend to be shorter than normal ones. Abstraction also helps learning by enabling chunks to be more general than they would otherwise be—the chunks ignore the details that were abstracted away—thus allowing more transfer and potentially decreasing the cost of matching the chunks (because there are now fewer conditions) [Rosenbloom, Laird, Newell, and McCarl, 1991, pp. 313—314, italics added].

SOAR: Scope and Limits

Rosenbloom, Laird, Newell, and McCarl (1991) evaluate SOAR's progress and prospects in the following detailed discussion.

The original work on SOAR demonstrated its capabilities as a general problem solver that could use any of the weak methods when appropriate, across a wide range of tasks. Later we came to understand how to use SOAR as the basis for knowledge-based systems, and how to incorporate appropriate learning and perceptual motor capabilities into the architecture. These developments increased SOAR's scope considerably beyond its origins as a weak-method problem solver. Our ultimate goal has always been to develop the system to the point where its scope includes everything required of a general intelligence. In this section we examine how far SOAR has come from its relatively limited initial demonstrations towards its relatively unlimited goal. This discussion is divided up according to the major components of the SOAR architecture, . . . memory, decisions, goals, learning, and perception and motor control.

Level 1: Memory

The scope of SOAR's memory level can be evaluated in terms of the amount of knowledge that can be stored, the types of knowledge that can be represented, and the organization of the knowledge.

Amount of knowledge. Using current technology, SOAR's production memory can support the storage of thousands of independent chunks of knowledge. The size is primarily limited by the cost of processing larger numbers of productions. Faster machines, improved match algorithms and parallel implementations [Gupta and Tambe, 1988; Tambe, Acharya, and Gupta, 1989; Tambe, Kalp, Gupta, Forgy, Milnes, and Newell, 1988] may raise this effective limit by several orders of magnitude over the next several years.

Types of knowledge. The representation of procedural and propositional declarative knowledge is well developed in SOAR. However, we don't have well worked-out approaches to many other knowledge representation problems, such as the representation of quantified, uncertain, temporal, and episodic knowledge. The critical question is whether architectural support is required to adequately represent these types of knowledge, or whether such knowledge can be adequately treated as additional objects and/or attributes. Preliminary work on quantified [Polk and Newell, 1988] and episodic [Rosenbloom, Newell, and Laird, 1990] knowledge is looking promising.

Memory organization. An issue that often gets raised with respect to the organization of SOAR's memory, and with respect to the organization of production memories in general, is the apparent lack of higher-order memory organization. There are no scripts [Schank and Ableson, 1977], frames [Minsky, 1975], or schemes [Bartlett, 1932] to tie fragments of related memory together. Nor are there any obvious hierarchical structures which limit what sets of knowledge will be retrieved at any point in time. However, SOAR's memory does have an organization, which is derived from the structure of productions, objects, and working memory (especially the context hierarchy).

What corresponds to a schema in SOAR is an object, or a structured collection of objects. Such a structure can be stored entirely in the actions of a single production, or it can be stored in a piecemeal fashion across multiple productions. If multiple productions are used, the schema as a unit only comes into existence when the pieces are all retrieved contemporaneously into working memory. The advantage of this approach is that it allows novel schemes to be created from fragments of separately learned ones. The disadvantage is that it may not be possible to determine whether a set of fragments all originated from a single schema.

What corresponds to a hierarchy of retrieval contexts in SOAR are the production conditions. Each combination of conditions implicitly defines a retrieval context, with a hierarchical structure induced by the subset relationship among the combinations. The contents of working memory determines which retrieval contexts are currently in force. For example, problem spaces are used extensively as retrieval contexts. Whenever there is a problem solving context that has a particular problem space selected within it, productions that test for other problem space names are not eligible to fire in that context. This approach has worked quite well for procedural knowledge, where it is clear when the knowledge is needed. We have just begun to work on appropriate organizational schemes for episodic and declarative knowledge, where it is much less clear when the knowledge should be retrieved. Our initial approach has been based on the incremental construction, via chunking, of multi-production discrimination networks [Rosenbloom, Laird, and Newell, 1988; Rosenbloom, Newell, and Laird, 1990]. Though this work is too premature for a thorough evaluation in the context of SOAR, the effectiveness of discrimination networks in systems like Epam [Feigenbaum and Simon, 1984] and Cyrus [Kolodner, 1983] bodes well.

Level 2: Decisions

The scope of SOAR's decision level can be evaluated in terms of its speed, the knowledge brought to bear, and the language of control.

Speed. SOAR currently runs approximately 10 decisions/second on current workstations such as a Sun4/280. This is adequate for most of the types of tasks we currently implement, but it is too slow for tasks requiring large amounts of search or very large knowledge bases (the number of decisions per second would even get smaller than it is now). The principal bottleneck is the speed of memory access, which is a function of two factors: the cost of processing individually expensive productions (the *expensive chunks* problem) [Tambe and Newell, 1988], and the cost of processing a large number of productions (the *average growth effect* problem) [Tambe, 1988]. We now have a solution to the problem of expensive chunks which can guarantee that all productions will be cheap—the match cost of a production is at worst linear in the number of conditions [Tambe and Rosenbloom, 1989]—and are working on other potential solutions. Parallelism looks to be an effective solution to the average growth effect problem [Tambe, 1988].

Bringing knowledge to bear. Iterated, parallel, indexed access to the contents of long-term memory has proven to be an effective means of bringing knowledge to bear on the decision process. The limited power provided by this process is offset by the ability to use subgoals when the accessible knowledge is inadequate. The issue of devising good access paths for episodic and declarative knowledge is also relevant here.

Control language. Preferences have proven to be a flexible means of specifying a partial order among contending objects. However, we cannot yet state with certainty that the set of preference types embodied in SOAR is complete with respect to all the types of information which ultimately may need to be communicated to the decision procedure.

Level 3: Goals

The scope of SOAR's goal level can be evaluated in terms of the types of goals that can be generated and the types of problem solving that can be performed in goals. SOAR's subgoaling mechanism has been demonstrated to be able to create subgoals for all of the types of difficulties that can arise in problem solving in problem spaces (Laird, 1986). This leaves three areas open. The first area is how top-level goals are generated; that is, how the top level task is picked. Currently this is done by the programmer, but a general intelligence must clearly have grounds—that is, motivations—for selecting tasks on its own. The second area is how goal interactions are handled. Goal interactions show up in SOAR as operator interactions, and are normally dealt with by adding explicit knowledge to avoid them, or by backtracking (with learning) when they happen. It is not yet clear the extent to which SOAR could easily make use of more sophisticated approaches, such as non-linear planning (Chapman, 1987). The third area is the sufficiency of impasse-driven subgoaling as a means for determining when meta-level processing is needed. Two of the activities that might fall under this area are goal tests and monitoring. Both of these activities can be performed at memory or decision level, but when they are complicated activities it may be necessary to perform them by problem solving at the goal level. Either activity can be called for explicitly by selecting a "monitor" or "goal-test" operator, which can then lead to the generation of a subgoal. However, goals for these tasks do not arise automatically, without deliberations. Should they? It is not completely clear.

The scope of the problem solving that can be performed in goals can itself be evaluated in terms of whether problem spaces cover all of the types of performance required, the limits on the ability of subgoal-based problem solving to access and modify aspects of the system, and whether parallelism is possible. These points are addressed in the next three paragraphs.

Problem space scope. Problem spaces are a very general performance model. They have been hypothesized to underlie all human, symbolic, goal-oriented behavior [Newell, 1980]. The breadth of tasks that have so far been represented in problem spaces over the whole field of AI attests to this generality. One way of pushing this evaluation further is to ask how well problem spaces account for the types of problem solving performed by two of the principal competing paradigms: planning [Chapman, 1987] and casebased reasoning [Kolodner, 1988]. Both of these paradigms involve the creation (or retrieval) and use of a data structure that represents a sequence of actions. In planning, the data structure represents the sequence of actions that the system expects to use for the current problem. In case-based reasoning, the data structure represents the sequence of actions used on some previous, presumably related, problem. In both, the data structure is used to decide what sequence of actions to perform in the current problem. SOAR straightforwardly performs procedural analogues of these two processes. When it performs a lookahead operator to apply to a particular state, it acquires (by chunking) a set of search control productions which collectively tell it which operator should be applied to each subsequent state. This set of chunks forms a procedural plan for the current problem. When a search control chunk transfers between tasks, a form of procedural case-based reasoning is occurring.

Simple forms of declarative planning and case-based reasoning have also been demonstrated in SOAR in the context of an expert system that designs floor systems (Reich, 1988). When this system discovers, via lookahead search, a sequence of operators that achieves a goal, it creates a declarative structure representing the sequence and returns it as a subgoal result (plan creation). This plan can then be used interpretively to guide performance on the immediate problem (plan following). The plan can also be retrieved during later problems and used to guide the selection of operators (case-based reasoning). This research does not demonstrate the variety of operations one could conceivably use to modify a partial or complete plan, but it does demonstrate the basics.

Meta-level access. Subgoal-based problem solving has access to all of the information in working memory—including the goal stack, problem spaces, states, operators, preferences, and other faces that have been retrieved or generated—plus any of the other knowledge in long-term memory that it can access. It does not have direct access to the productions, or to any of the data structures internal to the architecture. Nonetheless, it should be able to indirectly examine the contents of any productions that were acquired by chunking, which in the long run should be just about all of them. The idea is to reconstruct the contents of the production by going down into a subgoal and retracing the problem solving that was done when the chunk was learned. In this way it should be possible to determine what knowledge the production cached. This idea has not yet been explicitly demonstrated in SOAR, but research on the recovery from incorrect knowledge has used a closely related approach [Laird, 1988].

The effects of problem solving are limited to the addition of information to working memory. Detection of working memory elements is accomplished by a garbage collector provided by the architecture. Productions are added by chunking, rather than by problem solving, and are never deleted by the system. The limitation on production creation—that it only occurs via chunking—is dealt with by varying the nature of the problem solving over which chunking occurs [Rosenbloom, Newell, and Laird, 1990]. The limitation on production deletion is dealt with by learning new productions which overcome the effects of old ones [Laird, 1988].

Parallelism. Two principal sources of parallelism in SOAR are at the memory level: production match and execution. On each cycle of elaboration, all productions are matched in parallel to the working memory, and then all of the successful instantiations are executed in parallel. This lets tasks that can be performed at the memory level proceed in parallel, but not so for decision-level and goal-level tasks.

Another principal source of parallelism is provided by the motor systems. All motor systems behave in parallel with respect to each other, and with respect to the cognitive system. This enables one form of task-level parallelism in which non-interfering external tasks can be performed in parallel. To enable further research on task-level parallelism we have added the experimental ability to simultaneously select multiple problem space operators within a single problem solving context. Each of these operators can then proceed to execute in parallel, yielding parallel subgoals, and ultimately an entire tree of problem solving contexts in which all of the branches are being processed in parallel. We do not yet have enough experience with this capability to evaluate its scope and limits.

Despite all of these forms of parallelism embodied in SOAR, most implementations of the architecture have been on serial machines, with the parallelism being simulated. However, there is an active research effort to implement SOAR on parallel computers. A parallelized version of the production match has been successfully implemented on an Encore Multimax, which has a small number (2–20) of large-grained processors [Tambe et al., 1988], and unsuccessfully implemented on a Connection Machine [Hillis, 1985], which has a large number (16K–64K) of small-grained processors [Flynn, 1988]. The Connection Machine implementation failed primarily because a complete parallelization of the current match algorithm can lead to exponential space requirements. Research on restricted match algorithms may fix this problem in the future. Work is also in progress toward implementing SOAR on message-passing computers [Tambe, Acharya, and Gupta, 1989].

Learning. In [Steier et al., 1987] we broke down the problem of evaluating the scope of SOAR's learning capabilities into four parts: when can the architecture learn; from what can the architecture learn; what can the architecture learn; and when can the architecture apply learned knowledge. . . .

One important additional issue is whether SOAR acquires knowledge that is at the appropriate level of generalization or specialization. Chunking provides a level of generality that is determined by a combination of the representation used and the problem solving performed. Under varying circumstances, this can lead to both overgeneralization [Laird, Rosenbloom, and Newell, 1986] and overspecialization. The acquisition of overgeneral knowledge implies that the system must be able to recover from any errors caused by its use. One solution to this problem that has been implemented in SOAR involves detecting that a performance error has occurred, determining what should have been done instead, and acquiring a new chunk which leads to correct performance in the future [Laird, 1988]. This is accomplished without examining or modifying the overgeneral production; instead it goes back down into the subgoals for which the overgeneral productions were learned.

One way to deal with overspecialization is to patch the resulting knowledge gaps with additional knowledge. This is what SOAR does constantly—if a production is overspecialized, it doesn't fire in circumstances when it should, causing an impasse to occur, and providing the opportunity to learn an additional chunk that covers the missing case (and possibly other cases). Another way to deal with overspecialized knowledge is to work towards acquiring more general productions. A standard approach is to induce general rules from a sequence of positive and negative examples [Mitchell, 1982; Quinlan, 1986]. This form of generalization must occur in SOAR by search in problem spaces, and though there has been some initial work on doing this [Rosenbloom, 1988; Saul, 1984], we have not yet provided SOAR with a set of problem spaces that will allow it to generate appropriate generalizations from a variety of sets of examples. So, SOAR cannot yet be described as a system of choice for doing induction from multiple examples. On the other hand, SOAR does generalize quite naturally and effectively when abstraction occurs [Unruh and Rosenbloom, 1989]. The learned rules reflect whatever abstraction was made during problem solving.

Learning behaviors that have not yet been attempted in SOAR include the construction of a model of the environment from experimentation in it [Rajamoney, DeJong, and Faltings, 1985], scientific discovery and theory formation [Langley, Simon, Bradshaw, and Zytkow, 1987], and conceptual clustering [Fisher and Langley, 1985].

Perception and Motor Control. The scope of SOAR's perception and motor control can be evaluated in terms of both its low-level I/O mechanisms and its high-level language capabilities. Both of these capabilities are quite new, so the evaluation must be even more tentative than for the preceding components.

At the low level, SOAR can be hooked up to multiple perceptual modalities (and multiple fields within each modality) and can control multiple effectors. The critical low-level aspects of perception and motor control are currently done in a standard procedural language outside of the cognitive system. The resulting system appears to be an effective test bed for research on high-level aspects of perception and motor control. It also appears to be an effective testbed for research on the interactions of perception and motor control with other cognitive capabilities, such as memory, problem solving, and learning. However, it does finesse many of the hard issues in perception and motor control, such as selective attention, shape determination, object identification, and temporal coordination. Work is actively in progress on selective attention [Weismeyer, 1988].

At the high end of I/O capabilities is the processing of natural language. An early attempt to implement a semantic grammar parser in SOAR was only a limited success [Powell, 1984]. It worked, but it did not appear to be the right long-term solution to language understanding in SOAR. More recent work on NL-SOAR has focussed on the incremental construction of a model of the situation by applying comprehension operators to each incoming word [Lewis, Newell, and Polk, 1989]. Comprehension operators iteratively augment and refine the situation model, setting up expectations for the part of the utterance still to be seen, and satisfying earlier expectations. As a side effect of constructing the situation model, an utterance model is constructed to represent the linguistic structure of the sentence. This approach to language understanding has been successfully applied to acquiring task specific problem spaces for three immediate reasoning tasks: relational reasoning [Johnson-Laird, 1983], categorical syllogisms, and sentence verification [Clark and Chase, 1972]. It has also been used to process the input for these tasks as they are performed. Though NL-SOAR is still far from providing a general linguistic capability, the approach has proven promising [Rosenbloom, Laird, Newell, and McCarl, 1991, pp. 314–321, italics added].

Commentary

SOAR is, at once, an advanced artificial intelligence system directed toward the emulation of human cognition, a theoretical and research tool for testing and integrating the data of experimental cognitive psychology, an empirical research program with foundations resting on the basic concepts contained on the physical symbol system hypothesis, a methodology that draws upon the concepts, techniques, and data of cognitive science, and ultimately a unified theory of human and artificial cognition.

8

Summary and Conclusion

In this chapter, the major themes discussed in the book are summarized and general conclusions are drawn.

The major themes and central components of the general unified theory of intelligence will be summarized by means of a table.

In Table 8.1 the logic of implication is foundation, bracketing conditional reasoning in the case of human intelligence and production rule in the case of artificial intelligence.

The table is organized into seven sections. Each section summarizes the generality of a major theme of intelligent reasoning as discussed in the book: Logical Implication (Chapter 1), Abstract Rules (Chapter 2), Discovery Mechanisms (Chapter 3), Analogical Mapping (Chapter 4), Explanatory Coherence (Chapter 5), Symbolic-Connectionist Models (Chapter 6), and the SOAR System (Chapter 7).

Validity of the General Unified Theory of Intelligence

The validity of the General Unified Theory of Intelligence is derived axiomatically from the validity of implication as the center of intelligence. Intelligent reasoning, mathematical and nonmathematical, scientific and every day, technical and nontechnical, literary and nonliterary, and deductive, inductive, creative, analogical, explanatory, symbolic, connectionist, reflexive or reflective, and human or computational, is a type of implication.

TABLE 8.1

General Unified Theory of Intelligence: Major Themes and Centralized Affect

I.   Logical Implication (Chapter 1)
     A.   Central Components
          1.   Conditional Reasoning
          2.   Production Rules
     B.   Major Applications
          1.   Mathematical Proof
          2.   Production Systems
          3.   Turing's Theory of Computation
          4.   The Psychology of Reasoning
          5.   Gödel's Theorem
          6.   Representation in Artificial Intelligence
          7.   Resolution in Artificial Intelligence
          8.   Psychological Content of Implication Statements
II. Abstract Rules (Chapter 2)
     A.   Central Component
          1.   Abstract Rules are Types of Implication
          2.   Used in Everyday Reasoning
     B.   Major Application
          1.   Permission Reasoning
          2.   Obligation Reasoning
          3.   Causal Reasoning
          4.   Statistical Reasoning (Law of Large Numbers)
          5.   Modus Ponens Reasoning
III. Discovery Mechanisms (Chapter 3)
     A.   Central Component
          1.   Sophisticated Production Rules (A type of implication)
          2.   Rediscovery of Scientific Laws
     B.   Major Application
          1.   Equations Discovered by BACON.3
               a.   Ideal Gas Law
               b.   Kepler's Third Law
               c.   Coulomb's Law

---

                d.   Galileo's Laws

                e.   Ohm's Law

     2.   Equations Discovered by BACON.4

                a.   Ideal Gas Law

                b.   Coulomb's Law

                c.   Snell's Law of Refraction

                d.   Black's Law of Specific Heat

                e.   Gay-Lussac's Law of Combining Volumes

                f.   Canizzaro's Determination of Relative Atomic Weight

IV.   Analogical Mapping (Chapter 4)

    A.   Central Component

        1.   Parallel Constraint Satisfaction Achieves Intelligent Mapping Between Source and Target Analogs

    B.   Major Application

        1.   Analogies Mapped by ACME

                a.   Lightbulb/Radiation Problems (Four Versions)

                b.   Fortress/Radiation Problems

                c.   Cannibals & Missionaries/Farmer's Dilemma Problem

                d.   Contras Interference

                e.   Politics Interference (Two Versions)

                f.   Water-flow/Heat-flow Explanation (Two Versions)

                g.   Solar System/Atom Explanation

                h.   Jealous Animal Stories (Six Versions)

                i.   Addition/Union

                j.   Attribute Mapping

                k.   Midwife/Socrates (Three Versions)

                l.   Chemical Analogies (Eight Different Analogies)

V.   Explanatory Coherence (Chapter 5)

    A.   Central Component

        1.   Evaluation of Competing Theories and Hypotheses

        2.   Evaluation Is Achieved by a Parallel Constraint Satisfaction Algorithm

---

B.   Major Application
    1.   The ECHO System Has Been Used for the Following
         Purposes
         a.   Evaluation of the Oxygen Theory versus the
              Phlogiston Theory (Lavoisier)
         b.   Evaluation of the Evolutionary Theory versus the
              Creationist Theory (Darwin)
         c.   Evaluation of Theories Concerning Extinction of
              the Dinosaurs
         d.   Evaluation of Theories Concerning Continental
              Drift
         e.   Evaluation of Problem Solving in Physics
         f.   Evaluation of Copernican Astronomy versus
              Ptolemaic Astronomy
         g.   Evaluation of Legal Reasoning
         h.   Adversarial Problem Solving
         i.   Perception of Social Relationships
         j.   Evaluation of Debate Between Newton and Decarr
VI. Symbolic-Connectionist Models (Chapter 6)
    A.   Central Component
        1.   Directed toward an Integrated Account of Both Strategic
             and Automatic Cognitive Processes that Constitute
             General Human Intelligence
    B.   Major Application
        1.   Holyoak (1991)
        2.   Holyoak and Thagard (1989)
        3.   Thagard (1989, 1992)
        4.   Shastri and Ajjanagadde (1993)
VII. The SOAR System (Chapter 7)
    A.   Central Component
        1.   SOAR uses Production Rules (A type of Implication)
        2.   SOAR Is Intended to Constitute, Eventually, a Unified
             Theory of Human Cognition

TABLE 8.1, continued

---

       3.   SOAR's Power Derives from:
            a.   Universality of Its Architecture
            b.   Uniformity of Its Architecture
            c.   Specific Mechanisms Built into It Are Its Architecture
            d.   The Coordination of Methods and Mechanisms within a Unified System
   B.   Major Application
       1.   All one-SOAR Computer Configuration System
       2.   The Cypress-SOAR Design System
       3.   The Neomycin SOAR Medical Diagnosis System

Scope of the General Unified Theory of Intelligence

The scope of the General Unified Theory of Intelligence is clearly depicted in Table 8.1. The scope will be extended as new major themes are identified beyond those in the table.

Limitations of the General Unified Theory of Intelligence

The major limitation of the General Unified Theory of Intelligence is that, although the central concept of implication will remain, the type of implication will need to be expanded and the generality of the major themes will have to be extended.

Appendix

Expert Systems and a General Unified Theory of Intelligence

Expert Systems: Generality of the Inference Engine and Problem-Solving Heuristics

As presented in this volume, the general unified theory of intelligence is centered on the unifying concept of the logical implication as manifested in human reasoning and production systems across major domains of cognition with special emphasis on the generality of cognitive processes within each of the domains: the generality of intelligent problem-solving systems, the generality of intelligent abstract rules, the generality of intelligent creative mechanisms, the generality of intelligent analogical mapping, the generality of intelligent explanatory coherence, the generality of intelligent symbolic connectionist models, and the generality of intelligence in the SOAR system.

In this appendix, a supplement to the general unified theory of intelligence that centers on the intelligence of expert systems is offered. There is a kind of unification of logic and a generality of problem-solving heuristics present in expert systems. Unified logic is inherent in the inference engine that is broadly applicable to many types of specific expert systems. The generality of problem-solving heuristics is demonstrated in that for a specific type of expert system, the heuristic used by the system and by the human expert are the same. Of course, insofar as an inference engine is a production system it can be subsumed under the general unified theory of intelligence as can problem-solving heuristics, which are specific applications of the general logic of implication.

Definition of an Expert System

A clear definition of an expert system is "an intelligent computer program that uses knowledge and inference procedures to solve problems that are difficult enough to require significant human expertise for their solution" (Feigenbaum, 1982).

Fundamentals of an Expert System

The two major components of an expert system are the knowledge base and the inference engine. The expertness of an expert system is confined to its knowledge domain. With respect to that knowledge domain (e.g., knowledge of infectious diseases and their therapy) its expertise is equivalent to that of a human expert diagnostician, but its general medical knowledge does not extend beyond the technical confine in which it was programmed. The expert system, by means of its inference engine, reasons in the same way as a human medical diagnostician by executing a series of inferences concerning diagnostic conclusions and therapeutic recommendations based on the nature of the patient's symptoms and differential patterns of disease syndromes.

Advantages of Expert Systems

Beginning in the 1980s, the use of expert systems has proliferated in the sciences, medicine, psychology, engineering, architecture, law, finance, and other professions; because expert systems possess a number of significant advantages and desirable features, the scope of their employment will expand in future decades. The economic advantage is that expert systems are less expensive than human expertise; they are reliable and do not show the degradation in performance that accompanies human fatigue, overwork, and stress; the power and efficiency of their expertise is quickly augmented by the introduction of new software, in contrast to the years of additional professional education required to augment human expertise; expertise is available by appropriate software and hardware anytime, anyplace throughout the world. Harman and King (1985) point to the advantage resulting from incorporation of the knowledge of many experts into the expertise of an expert system. Not only may an expert system possess deep knowledge, it may also display, in fine detail, a lucid explanation of the inferential reasoning it used to establish its conclusions; the validity of its expert advice can thus be verified or rejected.

Knowledge Engineering and Expert Systems

Knowledge engineering is the process by which expert systems are developed. The developmental process is cyclical. Over an extended period of time, the knowledge engineer gleans the experts' knowledge, encodes it in a program, revises it following a critique by the expert, and continues the process to its culmination where the expert system emulates the expertise of the human expert. The emulation includes the levels of certainty or uncertainty that characterize the expert's advice. Where certainty obtains, algorithmic encoding may be appropriate; but where knowledge or reasoning is uncertain, the expert system must be capable of heuristic or rule-of-thumb reasoning.

Knowledge Representation in Expert Systems

In an expert system, knowledge is frequently represented as rules (if, then statements). The knowledge and procedural rules are modular and behave like individual autonomous knowledge processors; the expert system thus resembles a parallel program. The knowledge in a rule-based expert system can easily be revised or expanded because the rules are modular. This adjustive capacity is important in order to accomodate the updating of data and the improvement of the explanation facility of the expert system whereby it describes and justifies its conclusions and recommendations.

MYCIN: The Classic Expert System

MYCIN (Davis, Buchanan, and Shortliffe, 1977) contains many original concepts and procedures that were fundamental in the subsequent flourishing development of expert system research, technology, and application.

MYCIN made the expert system truly rational by means of its explanation facility that supplied cogent reasons for its differential diagnosis of infectious diseases and appropriate selection of antibiotic therapies. MYCIN also pioneered in creating an expert system that could automatically acquire specialized information in a knowledge domain (Davis, 1979). The concept of a computer that could perform a didactic role as an intelligent tutor was originated in MYCIN (Clancey and Letsinger, 1984).

At the practical and commercial level, MYCIN contributed the concept of the expert system shell, in which the inference engine is a uniform component that can be used with a great variety of different knowledge bases. E-MYCIN (van Melle, et al., 1981) contained the essential shell or core that, following the removal of the medical knowledge base, could be filled with information from other domains of knowledge.

Expert Systems in Chemistry

Since the development of DENDRAL (Buchanan and Feigenbaum, 1978), the use of expert systems in chemistry has proliferated; research laboratories and industrial facilities regularly use these systems. The following is a list of the names of these systems and a description of their functions:

Name	Chemistry
CRYSALIS	Interpret a protein's 3-D structure
DENDRAL	Interpret molecular structure
TQMSTUNE	Remedy Triple Quadruple Mass Spectrometer (keep it tuned)
CLONER	Design new biological molecules
MOLGEN	Design gene-cloning experiments
SECS	Design complex organic molecules
SPEX	Plan molecular biology experiments

(Waterman, 1986)

Expert Systems in Electronics

In addition to applications in chemistry, expert systems are widely used for research and applications in the field of electronics:

Name	Electronics
ACE	Diagnosis of telephone network faults
IN-ATE	Diagnosis of oscilloscope faults
NDS	Diagnosis of national communications net
EURISKO	Design 3-D microelectronics
PALLADIO	Design and test new VLSI circuits
REDESIGN	Redesign digital circuits to new
CADHELP	Instruct for computer aided design
SOPHIE	Instruct circuit fault diagnosis

(Waterman, 1986)

Expert Systems in Medicine

Medical expert systems have a profound significance in research and in patient care:

Name	Medicine
PUFF	Diagnosis, lung disease
VM	Monitors intensive-care patients

ABEL	Diagnosis, acid-base/electrolytes
AI/COAG	Diagnosis, blood disease
AI/RHEUM	Diagnosis, rheumatoid disease
CADUCEUS	Diagnosis, internal medicine disease
ANNA	Monitor digitalis therapy
BLUE BOX	Diagnosis/remedy depression
MYCIN	Diagnosis/remedy bacterial infections
ONCOCIN	Remedy/Manage chemotherapy patients
ATTENDING	Instruct in anesthetic management
GUIDON	Instruct in bacterial infections

(Waterman, 1986)

Commentary

Perhaps the most interesting feature of an expert system is that it meets the often-heard criticism that human cognition is not primarily logical and algorithmic; that computers, therefore, provide poor paradigms for human reasoning; that computers do only what they are told to do.

However, expert systems, unlike conventional algorithmic programming where there is interweaving between the knowledge base and the inference engine and therefore a high level of rigid control, are characterized by separation of knowledge base and inference engine and by highly flexible controls. As a result, following input, their behavior is opportunistic, using heuristic reasoning to work through to an acceptable solution to an ill-structured problem, just as human experts do.

For highly structured problems with well-known procedural solutions, conventional algorithmic programming is appropriate. Where the human expert is working in an uncertain area or at the boundaries of known areas, however, inexact reasoning is used; the expert system emulates this trial-and-error reasoning behavior that is a function of heuristic experiential knowledge rather than logical and algorithmic knowledge.

The theory of fuzzy sets (Zadeh, 1965, 1988) permits the development of expert systems that model the inexact and ambiguous character of everyday human cognition. Traditional expert systems are based on bivalent logic (x is true or false). Fuzzy expert systems (Whalen and Schott, 1985; Zimmerman, 1985) are based on approximate logic (x is more or less true; x is somewhat similar to y; x is most of the time appreciably more effective than y). Thus, fuzzy expert systems can more closely simulate the natural analog character of the linguistic and reasoning behavior of the human expert.

References

Allen, S.W. and Brooks, L.R. (1991). Specializing the operation of an explicit rule. *Journal of Experimental Psychology: General, 120*:278–87.

Anderson, J.R. (1982). Acquisition of cognitive skill. *Psychological Review: 89*:369–406.

Anderson, J.R., (1983). *The Architecture of Cognition.* Cambridge, MA: Harvard University Press.

Anderson, J.R. and Belnap, N. (1975). *Entailment.* Princeton University Press.

Appel, K. and Haken, W. (1979). The four color problem. In L.A. Steen (ed.), *Mathematics Today: Twelve Informal Essays.* New York: Springer-Verlag, pp. 153–80.

Bartlett, F.C. (1932). *Remembering: A Study in Experimental and Social Psychology.* Cambridge, UK: Cambridge University Press.

BonJour, L. (1985). *The Structure of Empirical Knowledge.* Cambridge, MA: Harvard University Press.

Braine, M.D.S., Reiser, B.J. and Rumain, B. (1984). Some empirical justification for a theory of natural propositional logic. In G.H. Bower (ed.), *The Psychology of Learning and Motivation*, Vol. 18. New York: Academic Press, pp. 313–71.

Buchanan, B.G. and Feigenbaum, E.A. (1978). Dendral and Meta-Dendral: Their application dimension. *Artificial Intelligence, 11*:5–24.

Byrne, R.M.J. (1989). Suppressing valid inferences with conditionals. *Cognition, 31*:61–83.

Caudill, M. and Butler, C. (1990). *Naturally Intelligent Systems.* Cambridge, MA: MIT Press.

Chang, C.L. and Lee, R.C.T. (1973). *Symbolic Logic and Mechanical Memory.* Hillsdale, NJ: Erlbaum.

Chapman, D. (1987). Planning for conjunctive goals. *Artificial Intelligence, 32*: 333–77.

Chase, W.G. and Simon, H.A. (1973). Perception in chess. *Cognitive Psychology,* 4:55–81.

Cheng, P.W. and Holyoak, K.J. (1985). Pragmatic reasoning schemes. *Cognitive Psychology,* 17:391–4 16.

Cheng, P.W., Holyoak, K.J., Nisbett, R.E. and Oliver, L.M. (1986). Pragmatic versus syntactic approaches to training deductive reasoning. *Cognitive Psychology,* 18:293–328.

Cheng, P.W. and Juang, J. (1987). A parallel resolution procedure based on connection graph. In *Proceedings AAAI-87,* Los Altos, CA.

Church, A. (1956). *Introduction to Mathematical Logic.* Princeton, NJ: Princeton University Press.

Clancey, W.H. and Letsinger, R. (1984). NEOMYCIN: Reconfiguring a rule-based expert system for application to teaching. In *Readings in Medical Artificial Intelligence.* W.J. Clancey and E.H. Shortliffe (eds.), Reading, MA: Addison-Wesley, pp. 361–81.

Clark, H.H. and Chase, W.G. (1972). On the process of comparing sentences against pictures. *Cognitive Psychology,* 3:472–517.

Clocksin, W.F. and Mellish, C.S. (1981). *Programming in PROLOG.* Berlin: Springer-Verlag.

Collins, A.M. and Michalski, R. (1989). The logic of plausible reasoning: A core theory. *Cognitive Science,* 13:1–50.

Darwin, C. (1962). *On the origin of species* (text of sixth edition of 1872). New York: Macmillan.

Davis, P.J. (1979). *Circulant Matrices.* New York: John Wiley & Sons.

Davis, R., Buchanan, B.G. and Shortliffe, E.H. (1977). Production rules as a representation for a knowledge-based consultation system. *Artificial Intelligence,* 8:15–45.

Davis, P.J. and Hersh, R. (1986). *Descartes' Dream: The World According to Mathematics.* San Diego: Harcourt Brace Jovanovich.

DeJong, G. and Mooney, R.J. (1986). Explanation-based learning: An alternate view. *Machine Learning,* 1:145–76.

Dietterich, T.G. (1986). Learning at the knowledge level. *Machine Learning,* 1:287–315.

Dreyfus, H.L. (1972). *What Computers Can't Do.* New York: Harper & Row.

Duhem, P. (1954). *The Aim and Structure of Physical Theory,* trans. P. Wiener (first published 1914). Princeton, NJ: Princeton University Press.

Dyer, M.G. (1991). Symbolic neuroengineering for natural language processing: A multi-level research approach. In J. Barnden and J. Pollack (eds.), *Advances in Connectionist and Neural Computation Theory: Vol. 1: High Level Connectionist Models.* Norwood, NJ: Ablex, pp. 32–86.

Eddington, A.S. (1933). *The Nature of the Physical World.* New York: Macmillan.

Einstein, A. (1931). *Essays in Science.* New York: Philosophical Library.

Einstein, A. (1933). *The Method of Theoretical Physics.* New York: Oxford University Press.

Einstein, A. (1952). On the electrodynamics of moving bodies. In: H.A. Lorentz, A. Einstein, H. Minkowski and H. Wehl, *The Principle of Relativity.* Dover (originally published in 1905).

Ericsson, K.A. and Simon, H.A. (1984). *Protocol Analysis: Verbal Reports as Data*. Cambridge, MA: MIT Press.

Ervin, S.M. (1964). Imitation and structural change in children's language. In E. H. Lenneberg (ed.), *New Directions in the Study of Language*. Cambridge, MA: MIT Press.

Etzioni, O. and Mitchell, T.M. (1989). A comparative analysis of chunking and decision analytic control. In *Proceedings AAAI Spring Symposium on Limited Rationality and AI*, Stanford, CA.

Evans, J. St. B.T. (1977). Linguistic factors in reasoning. *Quarterly Journal of Experimental Psychology, 29*:297–306.

Feigenbaum, E.A. (1982). Knowledge engineering in the 1980s. Department of Computer Science, Stanford University, Stanford, CA.

Feigenbaum, E.A. and Simon, H.A. (1984). Epam-like models of recognition and learning. *Cognitive Science, 8*:305–36.

Fisher, D.H. and Langley, P. (1985). Approaches to conceptual clustering. In *Proceedings IJCAI-85* (pp. 691–97). Los Angeles, CA.

Flynn, R. (1988). Placing SOAR on the connection machine. Prepared for and distributed at the AAAI mini-symposium "How can slow components think so fast?" Ann Arbor, MI.

Fodor, J.A. (1983). *The Modularity of Mind*. Cambridge, MA: Bradford Books/MIT Press.

Fodor, J.A. and McLaughlin, B. P. (1990). Connectionism and cognitive architecture: a critical analysis. In *Connections and Symbols*, S. Pinker, J. Mehler, (eds.), pp. 3–71. Cambridge, MA: MIT Press.

Fong, G.T. and Nisbett, R.E. (1991). Immediate and delayed transfer of training effects in statistical reasoning. *Journal of Experimental Psychology: General, 120*:34–45.

Fong, G.T., Krantz, D.H. and Nisbett, R.E. (1986). The effects of statistical training on thinking about everyday problems. *Cognitive Psychology, 18*:253–92.

Foster, M. and Martin, M., eds. (1986). *Probability, Confirmation, and Simplicity*. Syosset, NY: Odyssey Press.

Genesereth, M.R. (1983). An overview of meta-level architecture. *Proceedings AAAI-83* (pp. 119–24). Washington, D.C.

Genesereth, M.R. and Nilsson, N. (1987). *The Logical Foundations of Artificial Intelligence*. Los Altos: CA: Morgan Kaufmann.

Gentner, D. (1983). Structure-mapping: A theoretical framework for analogy. *Cognitive Science, 7*:155–70.

Gentner, D. and Toupin, C. (1986). Systematicity and surface similarity in the development of analogy. *Cognitive Science, 10*:277–300.

Gödel, K. (1930). Die Vollständigkeit des axiome des logischen funktionenkalkuls. *Monatshefte für Mathematik und Physik, 37*:349–60.

Gödel, K. (1931). Uber formal unentscheidbare satz de principia mathematica and verwandter system, I. *Monatshefte für Mathematik und Physik, 13*:173–89.

Gupta, A. and Tambe, M. (1988). Suitability of message passing computers for implementing production systems. In *Proceedings AAAI-88* (pp. 687–92). St. Paul, MN.

Halford, G.S. and Wilson, W.H. (1980). A category theory approach to cognitive development. *Cognitive Psychology, 12*:341–56.

Halford, G.S., Wilson, W.H., Guo, J., Wiles, J. and Stewart, J.E.M. (1993). Connectionist implications for processing capacity limitations in analogies. In K. J. Holyoak and J. A. Barden (eds.), *Advances in Connectionist and Neural Computation Theory: Vol. II: Analogical Connections*. Norwood, NJ: Ablex.

Hammond, K.J., Siefert, C.M. and Gray, K.C. (1991). Functionality in analogical transfer: A hard match is good to find. *The Journal of the Learning Sciences*, 1:111–152.

Harmon, P. and King, D. (1985). *Expert Systems*. New York: John Wiley & Sons.

Harmon, G., Ranney, M., Salem, K., Doring, F., Epstein, J. and Jaworska, A. (1988). A theory of simplicity. *Proceedings of the Tenth Annual Conference of the Cognitive Science Society*. Hillsdale, NJ: Erlbaum.

Hillis, W.D. (1985). *The Connection Machine*. Cambridge, MA: MIT Press.

Holland, J., Holyoak, K.J., Nisbett, R.E. and Thagard, P. (1986). *Induction: Process of Learning, Inference, and Discovery*. Cambridge, MA: MIT Press.

Holyoak, K.J. (1984). Mental models in problem solving. In J.R. Anderson and S.M. Kosslyn (eds.), *Tutorials in Learning and Memory: Essays in Honor of Gordon Bower*. San Francisco: Freeman.

Holyoak, K.J. (1991). Symbolic connectionism: Toward third-generation theories of expertise. In K. A. Ericsson and J. Smith (eds.), *Toward a General Theory of Expertise: Prospects and Limits*. Cambridge, UK: Cambridge University Press.

Holyoak, K.J. and Koh, K. (1987). Surface and structural similarity in analogical transfer. *Memory and Cognition*, 15:332–40.

Holyoak, K.J., Novick, L.R. and Melz, E.R. (1993). Component processes in analogical transfer: Mapping, pattern completion, and adaptation. In K.J. Holyoak and J.A. Barden (eds.), *Advances in Connectionist and Neural Computation Theory, Vol. 2: Analogical Connections*. Norwood, NJ: Ablex.

Holyoak, K.J. and Spellman, B.A. (1993). Thinking. *Annual Review of Psychology*, 44:265–315.

Holyoak, K.J. and Thagard, P. (1989). Analogical mapping by constraint satisfaction. *Cognitive Science*, 13:295–355.

Hummel, J.E. and Holyoak, K.J. (1992). Indirect analogical mapping. In *Proceedings of the 14th Annual Conference of the Cognitive Science Society* (pp. 516–21). Hillsdale, NJ: Erlbaum.

Hunt, E. (1989). Cognitive science: Definition, status, and questions. *Annual Review of Psychology*, 40:603–30.

Hsu, W., Prietula, M. and Steier, D. (1988). Merl-SOAR: Applying SOAR to scheduling. In *Proceedings Workshop in Artificial Intelligence Simulation, AAAI-88* (pp. 81–84), St. Paul, MN.

Jepson, C., Krantz, D.H. and Nisbett, R.E. (1983). Inductive reasoning: Competence or skill? *Behavioral and Brain Sciences*, 6:494–501.

Johnson-Laird, P.N. (1983). *Mental Models*. Cambridge, MA: Harvard University Press.

Kaiser, M.K., Jonides, J. and Alexander, J. (1986). Inductive reasoning on abstract and familiar physics problems. *Memory and Cognition*, 14:308–12.

Kintsch, W. (1988). The role of knowledge in discourse comprehension: A construction-integration model. *Psychological Review*, 95:163–82.

Kline, M. (1980). *Mathematics: The Loss of Creativity*. Oxford, UK: Oxford University Press.

Kline, M. (1985). *Mathematics and the Search for Knowledge*. New York: Oxford University Press.

Kolata, G. (1993, June 24). At last, shout of "Eureka" in age-old math mystery. *The New York Times*, p. 1.

Kolodner, J.L. (1983a). Towards an understanding of the role of experience in the evolution from novice to expert. *International Journal of Man-Machine Studies, 19*:497–518.

Kolodner, J.L. (1983b). Maintaining order in a dynamic long-term memory. *Cognitive Science, 7*:243–80.

Kolodner, J.L. (1983c). Reconstructive memory: A computer model. *Cognitive Science, 7*:281–328.

Kolodner, J.L., ed. (1988). *Proceedings DARPA Workshop on Case-Based Reasoning*. Clearwater Beach, FL.

Kowalski, R. (1979). *Logic for Problem Solving*. Amsterdam: North-Holland.

Kulkarni, D. and Simon, H.A. (1988). The processes of scientific discovery: The strategy of experimentation. *Cognitive Science, 12*:139–75.

Kurzweil, R. (1990). *The Age of Intelligent Machines*. Cambridge, MA: MIT Press.

Laird, J.E. (1986). *SOAR's User's Manual (version 4)* (Tech Rep No. ISL-15). Palo Alto, CA: Xerox Palo Alto Research Center.

Laird, J.E. (1988). Recovery from incorrect knowledge in SOAR. In *Proceedings AAAI-88* (pp. 618–23).

Laird, J.E. and Newell, A. (1983). *A Universal Weak Method* (Tech Rep No 83-141). Carnegie-Mellon University, Department of Computer Science, Pittsburgh, PA.

Laird, J.E., Newell, A. and Rosenbloom, P.S. (1987). SOAR: An architecture for general intelligence. *Artificial Intelligence, 33*:1–64.

Laird, J.E., Rosenbloom, P.S. and Newell, A. (1984). Towards chunking as a general learning mechanism. In *Proceedings AAAI-84* (pp. 188–92). Austin, TX.

Laird, J.E., Rosenbloom, P.S. and Newell, A. (1986). Chunking in SOAR: The anatomy of a general learning mechanism. *Machine Learning, 1*, 11–4.

Langley, P. (1981). Data-driven discovery of physical laws. *Cognitive Science, 5*:31–54.

Langley, P., Simon, H.A., Bradshaw, G.L. and Zytkow, J.M. (1987). *Scientific Discovery: Computational Explorations of the Creative Process*. Cambridge, MA: MIT Press.

Langston, C., Nisbett, R. and Smith, E.E. (1991). *Priming Contractual Rules*. Unpublished manuscript, Department of Psychology, University of Michigan, Ann Arbor.

Larrick, R.P., Mogan, J.N. and Nisbett, R. (1990). Teaching the normative rules of choice. *Psychological Science, 1*:65–93.

Lavoisier, A. (1862). *Oeuvres* (6 volumes). Paris: Imprimerie Imperiale.

Leahey, T. and Wagman, M. (1974). The modification of fallacious reasoning with implication. *Journal of General Psychology, 91*:277–85.

Lehman, D.R. and Nisbett, R.E. (1990). A longitudinal study of the effects of undergraduate education on reasoning. *Developmental Psychology, 26*:952–60.

Lehman, D.R., Lempert, R.O. and Nisbett, R. (1988). The effects of graduate training on reasoning: Formal discipline and thinking about everyday life events. *American Psychologist, 43*:431–43.

Lewis, R.L., Newell, A. and Polk T.A. (1989). Toward a SOAR theory of taking instructions for immediate reasoning tasks. In *Proceedings Eleventh Annual Conference of the Cognitive Science Society,* Ann Arbor, MI.

Lucas, J.R. (1961). Minds, machines and Godel. *Philosophy, 36*:112–27.

Mannes, S.M. and Kintsch, W. (1991). Routine computing tasks: Planning as understanding. *Cognitive Science, 115*:305–42.

Marcus, G.F., Ullman, M., Pinker, S., Hollander, M., Rosen, T.J. and Xu, F. (1990). *Overextensions* (Occasional Paper No. 41). MIT, Center for Cognitive Science.

Medin, D.L. and Ross, B.H. (1989). The specific character of abstract thought: Categorization, problem solving, and induction. In R. J. Sternberg (ed.), *Advances in the Psychology of Human Intelligence, (Vol. 5).* Hillsdale, NJ: Erlbaum.

Medin, D.L. and Smith, E.E. (1981) Strategies and classification learning. *Journal of Experimental Psychology: Human Learning and Memory, 7*:241–53.

Miller, G.A. (1956). The magical number seven, plus or minus two: Some limits on our capacity for processing information. *Psychological Review, 63*:81–97.

Miller, G.A. (1962). Some psychological studies of grammar. *American Psychologist, 7*:241–53.

Minsky, M. (1975). A framework for representing knowledge. In P. Winston (ed.), *The Psychology of Computer Vision.* New York: McGraw-Hill.

Minsky, M. (1986). *Society of Mind.* New York: Simon and Schuster.

Minsky, M. (1991) Logical versus analogical or symbolic versus connectionist or neat versus scruffy. *AI Magazine, 12*:34–51.

Mitchell, T.M. (1982). Generalization as search. *Artificial Intelligence, 18*:203–426.

Mitchell, T.M., Keller, R.M., and Kedar-Cabelli, S.T. (1986). Explanation-based generalization: A unifying view. *Machine Learning, 1*:47–80.

Morris, M.W., Cheng, P. and Nisbett, R.E. (1991). *Causal Reasoning Schemas.* Unpublished manuscript, Department of Psychology, University of California, Los Angeles.

Newell, A. (1980). Reasoning, problem solving, and decision processes: The problem space as a fundamental category. In R. Nickerson (ed.), *Attention and Performance 8.* Hillsdale, NJ: Erlbaum.

Newell, A. (1990). *Unified Theories of Cognition.* Cambridge, MA: Harvard University Press.

Newell, A. and Rosenbloom, P.S. (1981). Mechanisms of skill acquisition and the law of practice. In J.R. Anderson (ed.), *Cognitive Skills and Their Acquisition.* Hillsdale, NJ: Erlbaum, pp. 1–55.

Newell, A. and Simon, H. A. (1972). *Human Problem Solving.* Englewood Cliffs, NJ: Prentice-Hall.

Newell, A., Rosenbloom, P.S., and Laird, J.E. (1989). Symbolic architectures for cognition. In M.I. Posner (ed.), *Foundations of Cognitive Science.* Cambridge, MA: MIT Press/Bradford Books.

Nilsson, N.J. (1980). *Principles of Artificial Intelligence.* Palo Alto, CA: Tioga.

Nisbett, R.E. and Wilson, T.D. (1977). Telling more than we can know: Verbal reports on mental processes. *Psychological Review, 8*:231–59.

Nisbett, R.E., Krantz, D.H., Jepson, D., and Kunda, Z. (1983). The use of statistical heuristics in everyday inductive reasoning. *Psychological Review, 90*:339–63.

Nosofsky, R.M., Clark, S.E. and Shin, H.J. (1989). Rules and exemplars in categorization, identification, and recognition. *Journal of Experimental Psychology: Learning, Memory, and Cognition,* 15:282–304.

Nowak, G. and Thagard, P. (forthcoming). Copernicus, Newton, and explanatory coherence. *Minnesota Studies In the Philosophy of Science.*

Osherman, D.N. (1974–1976). *Logical Abilities in Children Vol. 1 (2–4).* Hillsdale, NJ: Erlbaum.

Partridge, D. and Wilkes, Y., eds. (1990). *The Foundations of AI: A Sourcebook.* Cambridge, UK: Cambridge University Press.

Piaget, J. and Inhelder, B. (1958). Th*e Growth of Logical Thinking From Childhood to Adolescence.* New York: Basic Books.

Piaget, J. and Inhelder, B. (1975). *The Origin of the Idea of Chance in Children.* New York: Norton. (Original work published 1951).

Pinker, S. and Prince, A. (1988). On language and connectionism: Analysis of a parallel distributed processing model of language acquisition. *Cognition,* 28:73–194.

Polk, T.A. and Newell, A. (1988). Modeling human syllogistic reasoning in SOAR. In *Proceedings Tenth Annual Conference of the Cognitive Science Society* (pp. 181–87). Montreal.

Post, E.L. (1944). Formal reductions of the combinatorial decision problem. *American Journal of Mathematics,* 65:197–268.

Powell, L. (1984). *Parsing the Picnic Problem with SOAR3 Implementation of DYPAR-3.* Department of Computer Science, Carnegie-Mellon University, Pittsburgh, PA.

Pylyshyn, S.W. (1984). *Computation and Cognition: Toward a Foundation for Cognitive Science.* Cambridge, MA: MIT Press.

Quine, W.V.O. (1961). *From a Logical Point of View.* New York: Harper Torchbooks.

Quinlan, J.R. (1986). Induction of decision trees. *Machine Learning,* 1:81–106.

Rajamoney, S., DeJong, G.F., and Faltings, B. (1985). Towards a model of conceptual knowledge acquisition through directed experimentation. In *Proceedings IJCAI-85* (pp. 688–90), Los Angeles, CA.

Ranney, M. (1987). Changing naive conceptions of motion. Doctoral Dissertation, Learning, Research, and Development Center, University of Pittsburgh.

Ranney, M. (1993). Explorations in explanatory coherence. In E. Bar-On, B. Eylon and Z. Schertz (eds.), *Designing intelligent learning environments: From cognitive analysis to computer implementation.* Norwood, NJ: Ablex.

Ranney, M. and Thagard, P. (1988). Explanatory coherence and belief revision in naive physics. *Proceedings of the 10th Annual Conference of the Cognitive Science Society.* Hillsdale, NJ: Erlbaum.

Read, S.J. and Marcus-Newhall, A. (1993). The role of explanatory coherence in social explanations. *Journal of Personality and Social Psychology.*

Reich, Y. (1988). *Learning Plans as a Weak Method For Design.* Department of Civil Engineering, Carnegie-Mellon University, Pittsburgh, PA.

Rich, E. and Knight, K. (1991). *Artificial Intelligence, 2nd ed.* New York: McGraw Hill.

Rips, L.J. (1983). Cognitive processes in proportional reasoning. *Psychogical Review,* 90:38–71.

Rips, L.J. (1990). Reasoning. *Annual Review of Psychology,* 41:321–54.

Robinson, J.A. (1965). A machine-oriented logic based on the resolution principle. *Journal of the Association for Computing Machinery, 12*:23–41.

Rosenbloom, P.S. (1988). Beyond generalization at search: Towards a unified framework for the acquisition of new knowledge. In G.F. DeJong (ed.) *Proceedings AAAI Symposium on Explanation-Based Learning* (pp. 17–21), Stanford, CA.

Rosenbloom, P.S. (1989). A symbolic goal-oriented perspective on connectionism and SOAR. In R. Pfeifer, Z. Schreter, F. Fogelman-Soulie and L. Steels (eds.), *Connectionism in Perspective*. Amsterdam: Elsevier.

Rosenbloom, P.S. and Laird, J.E. (1986). Mapping explanation-based generalization onto SOAR. In *Proceedings AAAI-86* (pp. 561–67). Philadelphia, PA.

Rosenbloom, P.S., Laird, J.E. McDermott, J., Newell, A. and Orciuch, E. (1985). RI-SOAR: An experiment in knowledge-intensive programming in a problem-solving architecture. *IEEE Transactions on Pattern Analysis and Machine Intelligence, 7*, 561–69.

Rosenbloom, P.S., Laird, J.E. and Newell, A. (1987). Knowledge level learning in SOAR. In *Proceedings AAAI-87* (pp. 499–504). Seattle, WA.

Rosenbloom, P.S., Laird, J.E. and Newell, A. (1988). The chunking of skill and knowledge. In B.A.G. Elsendoorn and H. Bouma (eds.), *Working Models of Human Perception*. London: Academic Press.

Rosenbloom, P.S., Laird, J.E., Newell, A. and McCarl, R. (1991). A preliminary analysis of the SOAR architecture as a basis for general intelligence. *Artificial Intelligence, 47*:289–325.

Rosenbloom, P.S. and Newell, A. (1986). The chunking of goal hierarchies: A generalized model of practice. In R.S. Michalski, J.G. Carbonnell and T.M. Mitchell (eds.), *Machine Learning: An Artificial Intelligence Approach 2*. Los Altos, CA: Morgan Kaufmann.

Rosenbloom, P.S., Newell, A. and Laird, J.E. (1990). Towards the knowledge level in SOAR: The role of the architecture in the use of knowledge. In K. VanLehn (ed.), *Architectures for Intelligence*. Hillsdale, NJ: Erlbaum.

Ross, B.H. (1987). This is like that: The use of earlier problems and the separation of similarity effects. *Journal of Experimental Psychology: Learning, Memory, and Cognition, 13*:629–39.

Rumelhart, D.E. and McClelland, J.L. (1987). Learning the past tenses of English verbs: Implicit rules or parallel distributed processing. In B. MacWhinney (ed.), *Mechanisms of Language Acquisition*. Hillsdale, NJ: Erlbaum.

Rumelhart, D.E., McClelland, J.L. and the PDP Research Group, eds. (1986). *Parallel Distributed Processing: Explorations in the Microstructure of Cognition 1: Foundations*. Cambridge, MA: MIT Press/Bradford Books.

Sacerdoti, E.D. (1974). Planning in a hierarchy of abstraction spaces. *Artificial Intelligence, 5*:115–135.

Saul, R.H. (1984). *A SOAR2 Implementation of Version-Space Inductive Learning*. Computer Science Department, Carnegie-Mellon University, Pittsburgh, PA.

Schank, P. and Ranney, M. (1991). The psychological fidelity of ECHO: Modeling an experimental study of explanatory coherence. In *Proceedings of 13th Annual Conference of the Cognitive Science Society* (pp. 892–97). Hillsdale, NJ: Erlbaum.

Schank, P. and Ranney, M. (1992). Accessing explanatory coherence. In *Proceedings of the 14th Annual Conference of the Cognitive Science Society* (pp. 599–604). Hillsdale, NJ: Erlbaum.

Schank, R. (1982). *Dynamic Memory: A Theory of Reminding and Learning in Computers and People*. Cambridge, UK: Cambridge University Press.

Schank, R. and Ableson, R. (1977). *Scripts, Plans, Goals, and Understanding*. Hillsdale, NJ: Erlbaum.

Shastri, L. and Ajjangadde, V. (1993). From simple associations to systematic reasoning: A connectionist representation of rules, variables and dynamic bindings. *Behavior and Brain Sciences, 16*:118–129.

Smith, E.E., Lanston, C. and Nisbett, R.E. (1992). The case for rules in reasoning. *Cognitive Science, 16*:1–40.

Smolensky, P. (1988). On the proper treatment of connectionism. *Behavioral and Brain Sciences, 11*, 1–23.

Spellman, R.M. and Holyoak, K.J. (1992). If Saddam is Hitler then who is George Bush? Analogical mapping between systems of social roles. *Journal of Personality and Social Psychology, 62*:913–33.

Steier, D. (1987). Cypress-SOAR: A case study in search and learning in algorithm design. In *Proceedings IJCAI-87* (pp. 327–330). Milan, Italy.

Steier, D., Laird, J.E., Newell, A., Rosenbloom, P.S., Flynn, R., Goldirig, A., Polk, T.A., Shivers, O.G., Unruh, A. and Yost, G.R. (1987). Varieties of learning in SOAR, 1987. In P. Langley (ed.), *Proceedings Fourth International Workshop on Machine Learning* (pp. 300–311). Irvine, CA.

Steier, D. and Newell, A. (1988). Integrating multiple sources of knowledge in Designer-SOAR: An automatic algorithm designer. In *Proceedings AAAI-88* (pp. 8–13). St. Paul, MN.

Stenning, K. and Levy, J. (1988). Knowledge-rich solutions to the binding problem: A simulation of some human computational mechanisms. *Knowledge Based Systems, 1*:143–52.

Stenning, K. and Oaksford, M. (1993). Rational reasoning and human implementation of logics. In K. I. Manktelow and D. E. Over (eds.), *Rationality*. London: Routledge.

Stenning, K., Shepherd, M. and Levy, J. (1988). On the construction of representations for individuals from descriptions in text. *Language and Cognitive Processes, 2*:129–64.

Sternberg, R.L. (1990). *Metaphors of Mind: Conceptions of the Nature of Intelligence*. Cambridge, UK: Cambridge University Press.

Tambe, M. (1988). *Speculations on the computational effects of chunking*. School of Computer Science, Carnegie-Mellon University, Pittsburgh, PA.

Tambe, M., Acharya, A. and Gupta, A. (1989). *Implementation of production systems on message passing computers: Simulation results and analysis* (Tech Rep No CMU-CS-89-129). School of Computer Science, Carnegie-Mellon University, Pittsburgh, PA.

Tambe, M., Kalp, D., Gupta, A., Forgy, C.L., Miles, B. and Newell, A. (1988). SOAR/PSM-E: Investigating mass parallelism in a learning production system. In *Proceedings ACM/SIGPLAN Symposium on Parallel Programming: Experience With Applications, Languages, and Systems* (pp. 146–61). Atlanta, GA.

Tambe, M. and Newell, A. (1988). Some chunks are expensive. In J. Laird (ed.), *Proceedings Fifth International Conference on Machine Learning* (pp. 451–58). Ann Arbor, MI.

Thagard, P. (1978). The best explanation: Criteria for theory choice. *Journal of Philosophy*, 75:76–92.

Thagard, P. (1988a). *Computational Philosophy of Science*. Cambridge, MA: Cambridge University Press.

Thagard, P. (1988b). Dimensions of analogy. In D. Helman (ed.), *Analogical Reasoning*. Dordrecht, Holland: Kluwer.

Thagard, P. (1989). Explanatory coherence. *Behavioral and Brain Sciences*, 12:435–67.

Thagard, P. (1992). *Conceptual Revolutions*. NJ: Princeton University Press. Princeton.

Thagard, P. (in press). The conceptual structure of the chemical revolution. *Philosophy of Science*.

Thagard, P. and Nowak, G. (1988). The explanatory coherence of continental drift. In A. Fine and J. Leplin (eds.), *PSA 1988 (Vol. 1, pp. 118–26)*. East Lansing, MI: Philosophy of Science Association.

Thagard, P., Holyoak, K.J., Nelson, G. and Gochfeld, D. (1989). *Analog Retrieval by Constraint Satisfaction*. Unpublished manuscript, Cognitive Science Laboratory, Princeton University, Princeton, NJ.

Turing, A. (1950). Computing machinery and intelligence. Mind, 59, 434–60.

Turing, A.M. (1936). On computable numbers, with an application to Entscheuding's problem. *Proceedings of the London Mathematics Society, 52*:230–65.

Tweney, R.D. (1990). Five questions for computationalists. In J. Shrager and P. Langley (eds.), *Computational Models of Scientific Discovery and Theory Formation*. San Mateo, CA: Morgan Kaufmann, pp. 471–84.

Unruh, A. and Rosenbloom, P.S. (1989). Abstraction in problem solving and learning. In *Proceedings IJCAI-89*, Detroit, MI.

Unruh, A., Rosenbloom, P.S. and Laird, J.E. (1987). Dynamic abstraction problem solving in SOAR. In *Proceedings Third Annual Aerospace Applications of Artificial Intelligence Conference* (pp. 245–56). Dayton, OH.

van Melle, W., Scott, A.C., Bennett, J.S. and Peairs, M.A. (1981). *The EMYCIN Manual*. Tech. Report, Heuristic Programming Project, Stanford University, California.

Wagman, M. (1978). The comparative effects of didactic correction and self-contradiction on fallacious scientific and personal reasoning. *Journal of General Psychology*, 99:67–80.

Wagman, M. (1979). Systematic dilemma counseling: Theory, method, research. *Psychological Reports*, 44:55–72.

Wagman, M. (1980). PLATO DCS, an interactive computer system for personal counseling. *Journal of Counseling Psychology*, 27:16–30.

Wagman, M. (1983). A factor analytic study of the psychological implications of the computer for the individual and society. *Behavior Research Methods and Instrumentation*, 15:413–19.

Wagman, M. (1984a). *The Dilemma and the Computer: Theory, Research, and Applications to Counseling Psychology*. New York: Praeger.

Wagman, M. (1984b). Using computers in personal counseling. *Journal of Counseling and Development*, 63:172–76.

Wagman, M. (1988). *Computer Psychotherapy Systems: Theory and Research Foundations.* New York: Gordon & Breach Science Publishers.

Wagman, M. (1991a). *Artificial Intelligence and Human Cognition: A Theoretical Intercomparison of Two Realms of Intellect.* Westport, CT: Praeger.

Wagman, M. (1991b). *Cognitive Psychology and Artificial Intelligence: Toward a General Theory of Human and Artificial Intelligence.* Westport, CT: Praeger.

Wagman, M. (1993). *Cognitive Psychology and Artificial Intelligence: Theory and Research in Cognitive Science.* Westport, CT: Praeger.

Wagman, M. (1995). *The Sciences of Cognition: Theory and Research in Psychology and Artificial Intelligence.* Westport, CT: Praeger.

Whalen, T. and Schott, B. (1985). Alternative logics for approximate reasoning in expert systems: a comparative study. *International Journal of Man-Machine Studies, 1,* 19–33.

Washington, R. and Rosenbloom, P.S. (1988). *Applying Problem Solving and Learning to Diagnosis.* Stanford, CA: Stanford University Press.

Wason, P.C. (1966). Reasoning. In B. Foss (ed.), *New Horizons in Psychology.* Harmondsworth, UK: Penguin Books.

Waterman, D.A. (1986). *A Guide to Expert Systems.* Reading, MA: Addison-Wesley.

Weismeyer, M. (1988). *SOAR I/O Reference Manual, Version 2.* University of Michigan, Ann Arbor, MI.

Weismeyer, M. (1989). *New and Improved SOAR I/O.* Department of EECS. University of Michigan, Ann Arbor, MI.

Whewell, W. (1967). *The Philosophy of the Inductive Sciences* (first published in 1840). Johnson Reprint.

Zadeh, L.A. (1965). Fuzzy sets. *Information and Control,* 8:338–53.

Zadeh, L.A. (1988). Fuzzy Logic. *IEEE Computer, April 1988,* 83–93.

Zimmerman, H.J. (1985). *Fuzzy Set Theory and Its Applications.* Boston, MA: Kluwer-Nijhoff Publishing.

Author Index

Subject Index

About the Author

MORTON WAGMAN is Professor Emeritus of Psychology at the University of Illinois, Urbana-Champaign. Professor Wagman is a Diplomate in Counseling Psychology, American Board of Professional Psychology. He was honored as Distinguished Psychologist by the American Psychological Association in 1990.

Dr. Wagman is the originator of the PLATO computer-based Dilemma Counseling System. PLATO DCS, published by Control Data Corporation, has been internationally used at colleges and universities for research, service, and instructional purposes.

Dr. Wagman's research on computer counseling has been published widely in scientific and professional journals. Professor Wagman's most recent books are *Human Intellect and Cognitive Science: Toward a General Unified Theory of Intelligence* (Praeger, 1996), *The Sciences of Cognition: Theory and Research in Psychology and Artificial Intelligence* (Praeger, 1995), *Cognitive Psychology and Artificial Intelligence: Theory and Research in Cognitive Science* (Praeger, 1993), *Cognitive Science and Concepts of Mind: Toward a General Theory of Human and Artificial Intelligence* (Praeger, 1991), *Artificial Intelligence and Human Cognition: A Theoretical Intercomparison of Two Realms of Intellect* (Praeger, 1991), *Computer Psychotherapy Systems: Theory and Research Foundations* (1988), and *The Dilemma and the Computer: Theory, Research, and Applications to Counseling Psychology* (Praeger, 1984). Professor Wagman also wrote the article "Artificial Intelligence" for the *Encyclopedia of Psychology* (1994).

ISBN 0-275-95622-9

90000>

EAN

9 780275 956226

HARDCOVER BAR CODE